Basic Concepts In
MODERN DANCE

A Creative Approach

Basic Concepts In
MODERN DANCE

A Creative Approach

Third Edition

Gay Cheney

Professor of Dance
University of North Carolina — Greensboro

A Dance Horizons Book
Princeton Book Company,
Publishers
Princeton, New Jersey

© 1989 by Princeton Book Company, Publishers
© 1975, 1969 by Allyn and Bacon, Inc.

A Dance Horizons Book
Princeton Book Company, Publishers
POB 831
Hightstown, NJ 08520

Cover Design and Artwork by Eric Fowler

Photography: Dorothy Allen, Jan Jackson, Kenton Robertson

Photos thanks to the generosity of students and faculty of dance programs at The University of Southern California, California State University at Hayward, and The University of North Carolina — Greensboro.

Typeset by Photo Offset

LC # 88-60951

Editorial Coordinator: Richard Carlin

Printed in the United States of America

Library of Congress Cataloging-in-Publication Data

Cheney, Gay.
  Basic Concepts in modern dance.

  Rev. ed. of: Modern dance, 1975.
  "A Dance Horizons book."
  Bibliography: p. 109
  Includes index.
  1. Modern dance. I. Cheney, Gay, Modern dance.
II. Title.
GV1783.C44   1988   793.3'2   88-60951
ISBN 0-916622-75-4
ISBN 0-916622-76-2 (pbk.)

Contents

Foreword

The third edition of *Basic Concepts in Modern Dance* by Gay Cheney fills a special role in the literature in dance education. It is a comprehensive introduction to learning dance which makes the major areas of the art accessible for the beginner and novice.

The preface describes the book as a guidebook and the chapters proceed to set itineraries that involve the reader in a self-discovery of new ways of moving and perceiving. The first chapter sets the tone for traveling toward new experiences that grow easily from our own natural and familiar movement experiences. The journey starts with the familiar — our ability to move, to respond, to attend to sensation, and to feel. Next on the way the body instrument, its structure and its weight changes, is explored. A stop is made to introduce the abstract elements of dance — shape, volume, density, dimension, distance, floor pattern, direction, speed, rhythm, and energy — which connect the body to the means of making the art of dance. Chapters on choreography and performance map the way to move from exploration and improvisation to selecting and organizing the materials into performed dances. A section on self-evaluation helps the student reflect on responses and accomplishments in the previous travels.

Integral to each chapter are learning experiences for students to try on their own to explore each concept when presented and to give it personal meaning. Each experience has clear instructions for a movement response and directives such as "sense how it feels" remind the learner to be aware of new sensations and personal reactions. It is this combination of theory and the way it is interwoven with practice that makes this book valuable.

The author acknowledges that traveling is an individual matter by using the personal pronoun throughout the text. This speaks directly to the reader and individualizes the material. The learner is the focus of the book rather than the content which is the case with other dance education publications. This recognizes that knowledge and awareness of one's own body and its potential is the foundation for gaining technical skill and the basis for the creative process in dance. I have used this book with students and I found that it involves them more intimately with the ideas than the usual definitions, descriptions, and discussions of material presented in other dance publications.

The format of the book makes it particularly suited to beginning dance students in high school and college. It presents a comprehensive overview of the major concepts of the dance art with just enough material to sample but not so much as to overwhelm. For newcomers to the art form it says briefly and personally "This is what modern dance is all about!" This makes it a unique publication. Other books in the field either focus on indepth study of specific areas of dance such as improvisation, choreography or performance, or if they are more inclusive, they are directed toward teachers rather than students. The discussions and learning experiences provide homework assignments that can parallel the focus of a class or supplement a course as it develops over a semester.

The conceptual approach to dance as a field of study and an art is even more pertinent today than when the first edition was published. More dance educators and artists realize that dance has a theoretical base comparable to music and the other arts. Learning to dance is more than refining movement skills; it is a holistic undertaking that challenges the mind and the emotions. The author always keeps this mind. She is also aware that we dance because it is a source of enjoyment and she stresses that the learner keep that in mind.

Mary Alice Brennan,
Associate Professor of Dance
University of Wisconsin-Madison

Preface

For the Student Traveler

A guidebook, says the dictionary, is a handbook of information for travelers. This guidebook is for you who are about to do some of the most fascinating traveling in the world.

For dance is traveling; dance is going; dance is movement; dance is motion. What distinguishes dance from other kinds of travel is its emphasis on the manner of going. Dance is concerned not with the gross act of getting from one place to another, but with the nature of its itineraries.

The traveler's experiences along the way shape the character of the journey. The student of dance has countless experiences which shape the course of study. In fact, experiencing dance is the only way to know it. No one can merely read a book and become a dancer. This book is not meant to suggest that, nor does it advocate that you substitute the guidebook for the guide. There is no substitute for a fine teacher.

Your teacher is someone who can help you understand the directions given for each particular journey and be sure you are following them safely and accurately. If you have any questions about any of the "learning experiences" in the book, ask for help from your guide. Remember that there should be no pain associated with these experiences. You should move along the journey easily and naturally, without harm along the way. If anything hurts, see your teacher, or let her or him see you before continuing. The "learning experiences" are sequenced so as to take you from simple to more complex dancing, and your trip through these challenges is intended to be comfortable and safe.

As the book maps out these experiences to demonstrate certain aspects of dancing to you, it is meant to be read in motion. Like the traveler, the dance student can make almost anything of these experiences. And if, like the traveler, the dancer comes home broadened by the journey, with thirst for travel not quenched but increased, with memories of the going alive in mind and body — then he and she will know what it is to have danced.

For the Teaching Guide

This guidebook, in its third rendering, offers experiences and information to the student that will be facilitated and expanded by the wisdom of your experiences and insights. It includes a new, brief, but comprehensive history of modern dance that is written to give context to the form modern dance takes today and perspective on the dance experience provided by the book. Your broader knowledge will fill in the gaps and enrich the reading for your students.

Various sections of the book have been expanded to include aesthetic perspectives of more contemporary dancers. Others have been clarified to reflect new development in the study of motion and dancers' bodies. Your continued education and the books listed in the updated source list will be important to further explanations of issues and answers to questions raised by your class.

Along with the expansion of the resource list to include new books and videotapes referred to throughout the book is an updating of photographs, replacing at least some of the 1970s looks in the previous editions. Our students then were wonderfully spontaneous, fresh, communal, while today they look very professional and extremely well-trained technically. My preference is to keep some of both qualities. Please explain to your students that some of this is history as well.

This book is intended to introduce many of the steps in the process of dancing from initial body awareness to final performance, so it will work as an accompaniment for one course or over the span of several courses, depending on how you are organized to proceed. It might serve you as the basic routing from which you would make many diversions, spend more time on side trips here and there, or expand on the included subjects. Students could read about and perform the suggested exercises on their own, so that they come to class having had a small taste of one aspect of modern dance. You could then expand and elaborate on this material as long as you think appropriate in class. Most certainly you will use this text as it works most effectively for you, on the basis of your own travels with this material.

Being intentionally general, the book is meant to introduce, to pique interest, rather than to provide all the information about all aspects of learning or teaching modern dance. Hopefully, the reading list provides sufficient supplement on any area covered within this text for traveler and guide to get more complete information about that which interests them. If there is more you need to know about music, accompaniment, lighting, staging of and for dance, your music and theatre faculty should be a wonderful resource. They can provide a gamut of information: from what music demonstrates or supports *rondo* or *theme and variation* forms to what kind of lamp creates a soft diffused light on stage. Take advantage of the knowledge of specialists in your home, school, or town.

May this book be a helpful and supportive companion on this trip, and may its words, experiences, and images move with you easily as a good dancing partner ought to do.

Gay Cheney

1

The Story of Modern Dance

CONCEPT: History explains to us why we are here now and points the way toward the future.

The story of modern dance is not unlike the tale you are about to unfold for yourselves. It begins as a choice to move away from the rules, structures, and ideas of the past, those belonging to other ages and cultures of people, and to move towards a more individually creative theory of dance. John Martin, dance historian, has described modern dance as a "point of view" being different for every decade, every country, every human who gives birth to it. The new dancers of the turn of the century chose to release the past, tune in to the present, and totally redefine the idea of what dance is.

Some of you may be students of ballet and love the security of the positions, steps, and attitude that is clear, definite, and consistent for that form. You may love this form and use it as a strong foundation to support your new experiences, as a home to return to from travels down other paths. Hopefully, you are open and adventurous enough to take these new paths. Others of you may have tried to conform to the particulars of ballet and decided that you wanted a different, freer, more self-defining approach to dance. And still others may always have been in an atmosphere of creative, more individualistic approaches to dance: many people tell me they dance in their own living rooms with shades drawn, that they danced freely in the woods or on the beach as children. This is not to say that modern dance is without rules and forms. Each modern dance artist who has come along has developed a personal style of dancing and therefore a way of preparing people to dance their dances. But there are many different ideas about dancing and ways to prepare for it, so you will see as many different "points of view" about dance as there are people making dances.

It all began at the turn of the century, and what a wonderfully exciting time it was in so many ways. The spirit of change and revolution was in the air and contagious among people in many different areas of dance and art. Towards the end of the 19th century, revolutionary changes occurred throughout the world of creative art. Musicians were finding new sounds and structures in music, while artists were discovering new things to paint about and new ways to paint them. Even ballet underwent a great upheaval in the early 1900s as Serge Diaghilev, a powerful theatrical entrepreneur in Paris, gathered the talents of Michel Fokine and Vaslav Nijinsky, Igor Stravinsky and Erik Satie, Jean Cocteau and Pablo Picasso for the making of new and quite revolutionary ballets, often growing out of some of the most marvelous collaborations in the history of the theatre. Fokine reformed ballet choreography and Nijinsky made a startling new movement vocabulary available to ballet through such works as *L'après-midi d'un faune* (Afternoon of a Faun) and *Le sacre du printemps* (Rite of Spring). This may whet your appetite to read further about *Parade*, a Diaghilev production choreographed by Leonide Massine to music of Satie with cubist set and costumes designed by Picasso.

This modernist work was going on in Paris from the early 1900s to 1920s while the flapper era was in full swing in the United States. Jazz was coming into being as a popular music form and Vernon and Irene Castle became the darlings of society, introducing new social dances to the ragtime music. Through the 19th century, women had been laden with long and heavy dresses and full heads of hair; dancers were equally hampered by conventions of fashion. In the 1920s, Irene Castle bobbed her hair and shortened her skirt, popularizing a style that relieved women in all roles — housewife or ballerina — and freed legs and torsos to engage in a much wider range of movements.

Not only was the social scene changing as America outgrew her Victorian attitudes about body and dress and therefore dance, but events on stage also looked very different. Florenz Ziegfeld, the famous vaudeville producer, presented formations of gorgeous dancing girls chosen for shape of limb as well as quality of training. Four women who appeared in vaudeville as a beginning showcase for their particular talents are sometimes known as the originators of modern dance, certainly as "new" dancers, and occasionally as "aesthetic" dancers. They were strong women determined to make their individual artistic statement in dance outside of the conventions of ballet.

In the 1890s, Loie Fuller (1862-1928) went in search of more natural movement and explored dance in relation to the theatrical elements, inventing fantastic "Fire" and "Serpentine" dances, costumed in yards of rippling silk, illuminated by multicolored lights and occasionally by full moonlight for special effect. You will see images of Loie Fuller in sculptures, lamps, and pedestals in the Art Nouveau style, honored as a revolutionary in art and the originator of a new dance form. Loie toured extensively in Europe, which was more open to the freshness of American dance than her native land. She organized the first European tours of Isadora Duncan and Maude Allan in the early 1900s.

Isadora Duncan (1877-1927) is probably the best known of the early modern dancers, being the romantic subject of books and films that celebrated her free spirit, pioneering not only "free" dances but a totally liberated way of life.

Isadora's dances reflected the natural rhythms and movements of waves and trees. She was known for self-expressive improvisations to the music of classical composers like Beethoven and Chopin, ranging from the lyrical to the impassioned. Many of our images of Isadora's dances come from descriptions in books about her. The dances, or simulations of them, were also passed down from choreographer/teacher to student, and some current companies, like the Repertory Dance Theatre of Salt Lake City, Utah, have some of these early dances in their performing repertoire.

Maude Allan and Ruth St. Denis were concerned with form as well as freedom and actually choreographed dances that were repeated in the same way with each performance. Like Isadora, Maude Allan (1873-1956) was devoted to the simplicity of classical Greek art while St. Denis (1879-1968) was attracted by the exotic mysticism of the Orient, performing "Radha," "Incense," and "Nautch" dances with the flavor, costumes, and candles of India.

The flurry of excitement over the dance of these women set American dancing "free" or "aesthetic dance" on the front lawns of our homes and in the gymnasiums of our schools. Physical education teachers brought dance into college programs as a part of their curriculum. As more people experienced dance in the schools and colleges, more people wanted to see dance on the concert stage. Eventually Duncan and St. Denis were lauded as artists of note who had changed the course of dance in this country forever.

As you can see, modern dance had its seeds in matriarchy, consonant with turn-of-the-century concerns for suffrage and rights of women. The partnering of St. Denis with Ted Shawn (1891-1972) began to bring balance to this strongly feminist beginning. Shawn was interested in ways of developing the body and movement ability of the dancer. He eventually formed a company of men in order to impress the favorable image of man as dancer on the prejudiced mind of dance audiences. The Denishawn School, founded by St. Denis and Shawn, was the first to educate dancers and develop choreographers, and from this school the acknowledged founders of modern dance evolved. Modern dance as a serious art form, having an artistic philosophy to guide it, a movement principle to support it, and a unique and significant statement to be made by each of its proponents, developed out of Denishawn.

The seeds of artistic revolution were not limited to the United States. As Diaghilev was turning heads in France, Mary Wigman (1886-1973) was fascinating audiences in Germany. Wigman was the student of two men who were exploring movement in a more scientific way: Emile Jaques-Dalcroze was teaching musicians about rhythm by translating sound into movement; Rudolf von Laban was developing a theory of movement and a system of analyzing it that later developed into the most popular of movement languages — Labanotation — used to write out or record choreographies. Wigman studied with both Dalcroze and Laban, tempering their more scientific approaches with her own emotional involvement with dance, resulting in powerful and dramatic solo and group dances. Wigman influenced the dance of the United States when she toured in this country in the 1930s.

As both art and science began to make strong contributions to the development of concert dance in this country, it is no surprise that dance in education was similarly influenced. In 1916, the Physical Education Department of the University of Wisconsin at Madison sent a young teacher, Margaret H'Doubler, to New York to learn about the new dance and bring it back for inclusion in their program. H'Doubler worked with two significant teachers at Columbia University in New York City. She studied "natural dance," a creative dance based on natural movement developed by Gertrude Colby, and the science of movement, a system in which movement originated in the torso, devised by Bird Larson.

H'Doubler returned to the University of Wisconsin enthused with this wonderful synthesis of creative and scientific approaches to dance, and established the first highly developed dance program in education, with the first actual major in dance, in 1926. H'Doubler's contributions include some of the first serious writings on dance in art and education, and the oft-quoted philosophy that every child has as much right to be educated in dance and art as in spelling and arithmetic. Thus the values of educational theorists began to shift from prioritizing "the basics" to the understanding of art as basic to a student's total education.

The history of concert dance continued with the Denishawn and Wigman Schools sending forth four of the most influential modern dance artists: Martha Graham, Doris Humphrey, Charles Weidman, and Hanya Holm. They had a clear vision of the kind of dance they wanted to make and the kind of dancers they needed to perform it effectively.

Martha Graham (b. 1894) is perhaps the most famous of all modern dancers. Her career as choreographer, dancer, and teacher spans over 60 years. Her dance celebrates both our primitive passions and our heroic accomplishments through strong, intense, and angular motion. Her theory is that movement arises from the pelvis and is reflected through the rest of the spine, arms, and legs. From this theory grew a highly structured and sequenced technique based on the contraction and release of the lower torso. It is widely taught today in many schools and studios.

She is the most prolific of choreographers, producing over 150 works that range from the powerful *Primitive Mysteries,* which launched her reputation as a maker of unique dance statements, to *Letter to the World,* a masterwork based on the poetry and life of Emily Dickinson, and one of the many dances Graham choreographed to celebrate the accomplishments of women. *Appalachian Spring* (with music by Aaron Copland) is an exuberant celebration of American pioneer life, while *Clytemnestra* and *Night Journey* are exemplary of Graham's interest in the more serious, often tragic, nature of Greek myths. Graham continues to be a strong fount of creative energy. Her company vividly demonstrates the power of her works, and her school gives significant training to dancers.

In the 1930s and 1940s, there was only one company that equalled Graham's in importance and influence: the Humphrey-Weidman company. Doris Humphrey (1895-1958) was one of this century's leading choreographers and dancers. In her best works, she combined a grasp of the intellectual basis of a dance with a depth of feeling and compassion for the human condition. Few equalled her ability to balance the soloist and the group, to provide visual balance and complex movement patterns on stage.

Humphrey's *Water Study* of 1928 is a group work performed without musical accompaniment. In its waves of energy that ripple through the dancers it presaged Humphrey's important theory of fall and recovery that was the basis of her technique. In *The Shakers* and *With My Red Fires,* two works of the 1930s, Humphrey explored two different relations of leader and group. *The Shakers* represents an integrated community, and the female leader/soloist inspires her congregation to greater intensity of religious experience and feeling. In *Red Fires,* the demonic female represents the fascistic impulses that were sweeping the world at that time, showing how a leader can exploit the emotions of a group. *New Dance* displays her mastery of time design, while *Passacaglia* gives evidence of her brilliant shaping of dancers in space.

Humphrey continued to choreograph through the early 1950s until her death in 1958. She served as artistic director for the fledgling José Limón dance company, and helped Limón shape some of his most famous works. Her book on composition, *The Art of Making Dances,* was the first of its kind and is still highly respected and much used by students of choreography today.

Charles Weidman (1901-1975) was Doris Humphrey's dance partner until her retirement, and in many ways her artistic and personal foil. While Humphrey's works were serious, Weidman's choreography was more humorous, punching holes in human foibles. Weidman was a master dancer and pantomimist, and his expressive abilities won him a home on Broadway as well as the serious dance stage.

Weidman's best-loved works were semi-autobiographical. *Flickers* satirized the world of silent movies, and the small-town mentality of early 20th-century America. *On My Mother's Side* and *And Daddy Was a Fireman* drew on Weidman's Nebraska roots, taking a loving and nostalgic look at a simpler world. His *Fables for Our Time* (1947), based on the work of James Thurber, provided an excellent showcase for his comic talents. After the dissolution of the Humphrey-Weidman company in 1944, Weidman continued to dance and choreograph until his death in 1975.

Hanya Holm (b. 1893), the last of the so-called founders of modern dance, is the only one not native to America. A student of Mary Wigman, she left post-World War I Germany and came to the United States to establish a Wigman

School in 1931. Holm gradually adapted the Wigman approach to the energy and space of her newly adopted country, and the look and subject matter of her new dances became very American. Holm's *Trend* (1937) is a dance that depicts a society being destroyed by its false values and eventually optimistically rebuilding. This sense of drama led Holm to work in the theatre, and she choreographed for several musicals in the 1940s through 1960s. Her work in *Kiss Me Kate*, *My Fair Lady*, and *Camelot* paved the way for recent musical theatre choreographers Jerome Robbins, Bob Fosse, and Michael Bennett.

Holm is also well-loved as a teacher. Her first assistant, Alwin Nikolais, learned much about the formal demands of composition from her. She became an institution at Bennington College, Colorado College, Mills College, and the American Dance Festival summer-dance programs. Many notable teachers and dancers have passed through her New York-based school or through these summer courses.

Thus, in the 1930s and 1940s, modern dance grew in strength and prestige through the thought, writings, and work of serious artists whose lives were totally devoted to making dances, performing them, and teaching students to dance in their particular styles. Most of the modern dance artists whose works moved us in the 1950s and 1960s were students of these four pioneers. Some carried on these traditions exactly, while others utilized them as the basis upon which to make their own individual statements. Still others reacted against these teachers, going off on their own new and revolutionary paths.

For example, Alwin Nikolais (b. 1912), student of Hanya Holm, teaches technique in the style of his mentor, organizing beautiful sequences of motion developed through shape, space, and time designs. But he has dropped the notion of emotional, self-expressive dances, and has gone on to create illusion and new reality through motion. Moving shapes become more than human through the use of fantastic costumes, properties, stage environments, and unusual sound scores, the combination of which makes for altogether magical events. In *Imago*, choreographed in 1963, the dancers' shapes are altered through cylindrical hats, extensions to their arms, and disks worn on the bottom of their feet. Later in 1960s, *Tower* and *Tent* included the building of these actual structures on stage for triumphant and thrilling effects.

The Nikolais aesthetic is a clean and powerful one, refining and simplifying the gestures of those who work with him. His sound teachings and eloquent speaking and writing have added depth to the consideration of dance as an art form.

As a student of Doris Humphrey, José Limón (1908-1972) adapted her choreographic principles for use in his strongly stylistic dances. His sense of formalism derived from Humphrey, combined with his own passion and emotionality, makes for powerful and moving choreography. A fine example of this blend is *There Is a Time*, based on themes from Ecclesiastes, which luckily is still available for our viewing on film and through the continuing performances of the Limón Company.

Limón's dancing was as significant as his choreography. Being schooled by Humphrey and Weidman, he performed as both partner to Humphrey and valued member of the company. His intense nature and strong stage presence led him to make his own dances where his expressive capabilities through movement, gestures, and facial expressions could come together to form memorable characterizations. It is no accident that his most famous works *The Moor's Pavane* and *The Emperor Jones* are based on strongly dramatic stage plays.

Limón developed a technique for training dancers based on the Humphrey style of fall and recovery, giving in to gravity and rebounding from the earth. A movement may be initiated in the ribs and then travel progressively out through the shoulder, elbow, wrist, and fingers, giving a smooth sense of flow. This flowing sequence of movements gives the Limón style a lyrical quality that is unique in modern dance. For students of dance, the Limón technique is often studied and enjoyed as a counterbalance to the Graham technique.

Anna Sokolow (b. 1912) began her career as a Graham dancer, and soon began choreographing on her own. Her early work reflected social issues of the 1930s and her own radical political philosophy. In the 1950s, Sokolow began focusing on human isolation and the existential plight of man in a modern industrial society. Her most famous work, *Rooms*, is an exploration of the psychological divisions, the "walls" between people. The use of a jazz score underscores the contemporary, urban feeling of this work.

Long a teacher at the Juilliard School, Sokolow has been influential in training many notable dancers, including Ze'eva Cohen and Jeff Duncan, both ex-company members. From the early 1960s on, her work has focused on melding dance with other theatrical forms to create a total theatre experience. She has also returned to her Jewish roots to create dances based on her unique heritage, and to encourage the growth of modern dance in Israel.

Erick Hawkins (b. 1909) is one of many fascinating figures in modern dance. Harvard educated, he studied Greek in college, and encountered modern dance, almost by accident, at small recitals. He enrolled at the fledgling School of American Ballet and became a ballet dancer with companies that were forerunners of the New York City Ballet. When his ballet company performed at the Bennington College Summer School of Dance, he met Martha Graham, soon renounced ballet training, and became a member of the Graham company.

Briefly married to Graham, Hawkins left the company in 1950 and took a new direction in his technique. Renouncing Graham's narrative thrust, he began exploring the underlying imagery of myth. His work is divided neatly into two strands: "pure" dances that celebrate human movement unfettered by any "meaning"; and more "narrative" works, which present broadly-painted stories, often based on primitive myths. In *Here and Now With Watchers*, Hawkins revels in the mystical side of his personality, offering snippets of narrative and echoes of myth, but primarily presenting pure movement with the flavoring of some undefined ceremony. In the humorous *Classic Kite Tails,* this exploration of movement-for-movement's sake is carried through to its fullest possibility. Hawkins has also created memorable dances using interesting masks and costumes. In *Plains Daybreak* (1979), he draws on American Indian myth, with each dancer portraying a different animal spirit and wearing a special head-mask that extends the body and is designed to reflect body movements.

Hawkins' technique is neither balletic nor Graham-like. It seems that he needed to take a strong stand on his own to define his own movement style. Hawkins draws heavily on his study of human anatomy, to work in harmony with the natural structure of the body to create a fluid movement style and fluent dancers.

Merce Cunningham (b. 1919) also performed for some years as a member of the Graham Company. You will see him dancing the part of the Revivalist in *Appalachian Spring* recorded on film. Upon leaving the Graham Company, he worked in a whole new way, being one of the first to challenge the theories of the founders of modern dance. Dropping concern for storyline and drama, as had Nikolais and Hawkins, he furthered the notion that dance is about movement and movement only, and that the meaning of movement is determined by the individual viewer rather than being given by the choreographer. To break from literal interpretations and expected sequences of movement, he employed Asian practices of chance to determine the order of events and the place on the stage where these events might occur. A toss of the dice might determine which dancer did what phrase of music, a flip of the coin decided what phrase started the choreography. To assure freshness and spontaneity, music, set, and costumes were added to the dance at the time of performance, never before seen or heard by the dancers, to insure that each ingredient had its own particular integrity and existence in performance.

In keeping with his aesthetic, Cunningham trained his dancers to render his choreographies in an emotionally detached way. His technique is known to be somewhat balletic, working for clean line and objective presentation of movement. Patterns are rhythmically complex and challenging, and often oppose the natural logic of movement progressions. The momentum of a leap might impel the dancer continually forwards; the Cunningham choreography might ask the dancer to take that impulse and pull it backwards instead or turn it sideways. The audience stays fully awake, and is unable to lean on comfortable and expected sequences of movements. The nature of the movement, the choreography, the last-minute adding of sound, costume, and set were all very challenging to the dancers as well as to the audience.

As you might well imagine, the ideas and work of Merce Cunningham gave rise to reactions of stern disapproval and strong arguments about the nature of art. But this is not unlike the response to all stages of the development of the thing called modern dance, not unlike the issues and questions going on in all of the arts all of the time. Is art a matter of self-expression? Is art about beauty? If so, what is beauty? Does art reflect or comment on reality? Or is art itself reality? Should dance tell a story that already exists, as in Graham's *Night Journey*? Or is dance its own story, as in Nikolais' *Totem*?

Cunningham was certainly not alone in his revolutionary concepts. John Cage, who worked with "found sounds" as the medium of music, composed scores or read poetry as the accompaniment to Cunningham's dances. If the dance was 17 minutes long, so was the accompaniment, otherwise there was no relationship between these parts. Robert Rauschenberg and Jasper Johns designed sets that were planted or that floated in the stage space and put costumes on the dancers, three minutes before the dance was performed. Cunningham, Cage, and Rauschenberg considered art a reflection of life: our lives are not logical, controlled, orderly. Things happen to us by chance all the time. We may have a plan but events happen that change and interrupt it continually. In reality, we do not control and design everything we see, hear, or feel. We look out at the street and see somebody we know walking along the sidewalk against a backdrop of moving cars, restaurants, and stores to the sound of traffic and car radios, fragments of music, and conversations. So why not make dances in the same way, they asked. On the other hand, art could be a reaction to this haphazard life with all parts carefully thought out, controlled, and organized exactly as we would like it to be, in the ideal, most beautiful form. What do you think art ought to be?

The worlds of concert dance and dance education proceeded in parallel but separate paths for some years. Ultimately, in the 1940s and 1950s, the meetings and interweavings were frequent and rich. College dance teachers studied in private studios and dance companies performed on college campuses. For example, at the University of Wisconsin, Louise Kloepper, performing member of the Hanya Holm Company, joined the faculty of the Dance Department, while Mary Hinkson and Helen McGehee graduated from the university and became performing members of the Graham Company.

The university dance departments developed dance studies in art, science, and philosophy, and sent many influential people out into the world. There were performers, choreographers, teachers of dance, and dance therapists who stretched our understanding not only of dance as a creative art form, but dance as a means of education and growth and as a way to self-knowledge and healing. While through the years many programs of dance appeared and flourished in departments of Physical Education, ultimately dance was housed in departments of Music and Theatre or existed self-sufficiently in Dance departments. Today there are colleges like Juilliard and the North Carolina School of the Arts that focus on developing artists, dancers, and choreographers, and there are high schools with art-centered curricula in which general studies are peripheral to that focus.

Learning Experience
Dance Magazine *has a* College Directory *that lists and describes the dance major programs in schools and colleges across the country. Scan this to get a sense of the breadth and variety of programs available to serious students of dance. Ask people who know about the differences between BFA and BS degrees, and about graduate study in dance.*

The 1960s brought radical change to the dance world. One movement developed out of a group of people taking a class in choreography with composer Robert Ellis Dunn at the Judson Church in New York City. It got down to the nitty gritty of questioning the nature of dance and dancers as well, not only the philosophy of art but its reality. Yvonne Rainer was the most "far out," saying "no" to all the things dance had formally concerned itself with: technique, virtuosity, performance, projection, meaning, beauty, drama, dynamics, phrasing, and form. Dance was seen as plain, simple, uninflected movement that could be performed with people watching, but not necessarily for their enjoyment or appreciation. Trisha Brown saw dance happening in all sorts of spaces and places outside the studio and theatre, and danced through miles of meadows in Connecticut, across rows of rooftops in New York, and up and down the walls of buildings with the help of various pieces of equipment, the reality of weight and gravity making for cumbersome and risky performances.

The question of training and natural ability was answered by Steve Paxton who did dances for 50 redheads he pulled in off the street, and Deborah Hays' circle dances performed with everyday people everywhere. While the Museum of Modern Art was showing a car that had been squashed and compacted for the wrecking yards, John Cage was opening the window for concert audiences to hear 7 minutes and 32 seconds of New York City noise, and the "postmodern dancers" were rehearsing untrained pedestrians in "found movement" sequences and organizing spontaneous "happenings" in many unusual theatre environments. Anna Halprin was frying eggs and climbing cargo nets on the stages of San Francisco, and Meredith Monk was observing spectators moving through the Museum of Modern Art in New York. We know the 1960s as a time of questioning everything. Hippies, flower children, and anti-war, anti-establishment, anti-art, anti-racism, anti-sexism, and anti-tradition philosophies were all thrown in the same bag. Everything was up for questioning, reconsidering, and revaluing. The world has never been quite the same since.

These same years focused attention on developments within minority groups. Black culture had been unmistakably the greatest influence on popular music and dance. Jazz, ragtime, be-bop, rock 'n roll, the Charleston, jitterbug, swim, watusi, and breakdancing all grew out of the full-bodied, free-spirited music and dance heritage of black people. But popular culture was one thing, art another. Not being accepted into white companies, black dancers organized to showcase their particular talents. Concert dance recognized and included the works of Katherine Dunham and Pearl Primus whose choreography reflected their pioneering studies of African and Caribbean traditional dance. Eleo Pomare, Talley Beatty, and Rod Rodgers based modern dance choreographies on the lifestyle, pain, and rage of black people in our society. Chuck Davis and Arthur Hall brought audiences into the dance/drumming ceremonies of various African nations.

Alvin Ailey (1931–1989) was one of the leading choreographers in modern dance. He began his career as a member of the Lester Horton company in California, absorbing much of his technique. After Horton's death in 1953, Ailey formed a new company, called the American Dance Theatre, with many of Horton's dancers, including Carmen de Lavallade, Joyce Trisler, and James Truitte. Ailey choreographed for Broadway in the 1950s, and more recently for ballet companies. He tried to find a middle ground between modern dance and ballet in his work.

One of Ailey's most famous works is *Revelations,* first performed in 1960. It has become a signature piece for Ailey's American Dance Theatre. Using traditional spirituals as its music, the piece consists of solos and group works that express the depth of black American life. *The Lark Ascending,* from the early 1970s, is set to a classical score by Ralph Vaughan Williams, and reflects a more lyrical side to Ailey's work, showing the influence of ballet technique on his style.

Through his school, Ailey has trained hundreds of modern and ballet dancers. Using Horton's eclectic training as a starting point, Ailey's technique creates dancers who are unusually strong, athletic, and versatile. Ailey dancers also have enjoyed long careers, without as much injury as other dancers, thanks to this thoroughgoing training.

As racial issues climaxed and integration became more fact than theory, it grew more usual to see companies of mixed colors and ethnic backgrounds. Billy Frank and Cora Martingale were particularly vivid shapes among the Nikolais dancers; Matt Turney and Mary Hinkson were particularly strong personages in the Graham dance-dramas; Gus Solomons, Jr., grew up in the nonliteral dance of Cunningham and continued this abstract style in his own choreography. The Ailey company tours internationally with a group of integrated dancers who perform lyrical ballets like *Lark Ascending* as well as dances based on black heritage.

In this day, the Bill T. Jones-Arnie Zane Company is well known for its inventive and interesting choreography. Under its black-white leadership, the company has made occasional social-political statements in dance, but more often does dances which are beyond racial/sexual heritage and stereotypes, and simply have to do with people dancing.*

In the late 1970s and early 1980s, postmoderns went as far out as they could and then came back somewhat closer to center. Steve Paxton developed a spontaneous communal form based on momentum and gravity and the taking and giving of weight called "contact improvisation." Trisha Brown's dances are often based on game rules and formulas, and include movements of specific quality that keep delighting and surprising audiences who cannot guess what will happen next and cannot stop paying attention for a moment. Deborah Hay still makes large group dances, choreographies derived from the *I Ching* and visionary images, with dancers practicing awareness of every cell and continuous presence in the moment. The videotape *Beyond the Mainstream* and Sally Banes' *Terpsichore in Sneakers* will give you much more information about this era of dance, a challenging and interesting one.

As much experimentation as there was during this period of the 1960s and the 1970s there was also the continuation of so-called "mainstream" modern dance that still conformed to some of the earlier traditions. The Graham and Limón companies continued to perform the work of their mentors and new companies sprouted out of similar or related traditions.

Paul Taylor is one of those whose background was with both Cunningham and Graham, and who also engages in some of the explorations of the postmoderns. Louis Horst published his now infamous "blank page" review in reaction to one of Paul Taylor's first dances, *Epic*, which presented a man in a business suit performing tight, restrained gestures to the accompaniment of a telephone recording announcing the time. This minimalist, purposely restrained work showed the influence of the New York avant-garde, but was totally baffling to the older generation.

By the mid-1960s, Taylor had pursued his own work and was recognized as a premiere dancer and choreographer, whose work combines athletic skill, humor, and a balancing act between comedy and tragedy. The dances suggest a narrative, without being tied down to literal "presentation" of a story. In dances like *Three Epitaphs, Scudorama,* and *Private Domain*, Taylor presents the human tragicomedy of relationships. *Scudorama* takes as its starting point a verse from Dante's *Inferno,* and presents scuttling and hurrying figures as symbolic of the incessant movements of human life. *Private Domain* also probes the meeting place between the private person and the public persona, and the need for relationships in a world often devoid of feeling. His work provides a new and

---

* Sadly, Arnie Zane died of AIDS in the spring of 1988. The company, however, continues to perform innovative works under its original name.

different way of dealing with dances which say things, dances which mean things but in a unique and subtle way.

As there are schools of thought and communities of ideas, so there are also companies of dancers who collaborate on making dances. Pilobolus was formed out of a group of students and a dance faculty member at Dartmouth College. Creative and innovative, this company is one of the most popular and entertaining groups existing today. Much of their dance-movement vocabulary is derived from gymnastics, mime, and creative stage movement. They seem to avoid purposely movements that an audience might recognize as coming from the mainstream modern-dance tradition in order to forge their own unique style. The dances themselves are based on myths, folk songs, and legends and often present endearing characters, such as the one Moses Pendleton created in *Momix*. Light, provocative, and persistent in memory, the images are sometimes hilarious and often delightfully bizarre.

In the 1980s, modern dance seems to have greatly decentralized. While the Ailey, Nikolais, Cunningham, Graham, and Limón studios continue their missions and their companies tour worldwide, a proliferation of small young individual companies survives. Some of this new work seems to have to do with energy, with pushing the limits of human endurance in sustained, continuous, and high-level energy output, in nonstop movement. Other times, dance seems transformational. The repetition of movement and/or rhythm in the Laura Dean dances and the meditational focus of the Deborah Hay dances have possibilities for taking dancers and audiences into altered states of consciousness. We watch Mark Morris of Seattle and Pina Bausch of Wuppertal with interest and note the return of dances that speak again of movement that means, of movement that tells us of certain feelings, attitudes, and points of view.

We know the world of dance is still open and growing, changing, dynamic, exciting, focused on the individual and what he or she wants to say in and through dance. And we look forward to who it is that you are and what it is that you have to say throughout this book and beyond, into whatever place you choose to go with dance: as choreographer or performer, as audience; as student, as teacher; as critic, author, therapist; as someone whose life and being is enriched by the dance experience. Happy journey!

2

Modern Dance and Movement

CONCEPT: Modern dance is an experience in movement.

1. Movement enables you to know your world.

Most of your basic knowledge came to you through movement. You first experienced yourself by the movement of your body. You first experienced your environment and other people by moving in relation to them. Feelings of satisfaction, frustration, love, fear, and pain were experienced through subtle changes of the body in movement. Concepts of space, time, and energy were learned as they related to your motion. You discovered the forces of gravity and momentum by having to move with and against them. Your first and last reactions to life, situations, and people are in the form of movement. This rich background should make dance a most natural activity for you. Many times, however, you may have developed attitudes about your body and movement that allowed you to let your movement awareness slip and to get out of practice using your own body meaningfully. It is hoped that this book will remind you of this natural process.

You know many things through your body from the many different life experiences that are registered in your muscles as memories. You know in your body what it is like to be in a crowd, to be in a hurry or in hesitation, in fear or joy, in a hammock or on the floor, in sunlight or shade. You know what it's like to be excited through the quivering of your knees, the quickness of your heartbeat, the busyness of your hands with each other. And you will know many other things through the feelings of your body, in the experiences yet to come. You will know your body in new ways, in new shapes and rhythms, in new tensions and energies. You will find yourself in new amounts of space, in new relationships with other people, with things, with lights, with shapes and textures. Whatever you experience, do it with your *entire* self, with your eyes and skin, mind and body, breathing and swallowing. Register each experience in your memory, and use it in the future with reference to your dances and your own further definition.

Dance is movement. Movement is life, and it surrounds you every moment. It attracts your attention in the form of flashing neon lights on busy streets, kinetic sculptures in museums, or rotating advertisements in shop windows. It fascinates you with animals, other people, racing rivers, and tangled traffic. You exist by means of it every day, from the earliest rising out of bed to the last flick of the light switch at night. Being alive means moving, and movement is the material of dance.

Learning Experience

Think of three things you learned (really understood, not just memorized) in the last year. What role did movement play in learning these?

---

2. The uniqueness of your body provides you with certain feelings about moving.

In many ways you are all alike. You have bodies with approximately the standard number of parts. You all have a shape, weight, height, size, and width. You have a torso, hips, shoulders, front, and back. You possess arms and legs, knees and elbows, hands and feet, eyes and nose — even *these* will dance.

The particular shape, size, weight, and height of your body — all the parts together — are what provide you with your individuality. This constitution is *yours*. There is none other quite like it in all the world. You need not be concerned with evaluating it in comparison with others or with any standard of perfection. It is sufficient to know that your body is different; what makes it different and unique makes up the quality of you. Know yourself realistically. Accept whatever part of yourself is unchangeable. You are not better or worse, but taller, shorter, rounder, more muscular, longer legged, heavier thighed, wider footed, shorter nosed than other people. You will know much more about yourself and the possibilities of your particular body as you go along.

3. Your body is you, and your realization of it is important.

Comparable with the sense of sight, hearing, and taste is a body wisdom called the *kinesthetic sense*. Through nerve endings in muscles and joints, this sense lets us know, without looking, what's going on down there in the big toe, tells us what the limit of our leg stretch is, and how a smooth, silky gesture feels in comparison to a jagged and craggy one. While we all have this ability to know what movement feels like through the kinesthetic sense, what we associate with those feelings is an individual matter. Depending on those associations, you will have different feelings about the movement, certain preferences. Some movements you find boring, only routine, while others you find quite satisfying, even exciting. You may feel at home in the hustle-bustle of a city, or you may prefer to sit and watch the subtle motion of change in the panorama of a sunset. You may feel at your best when engaged in vigorous action, or you may seldom move. You may like to run and jump, fall and rise; or you may enjoy merely changing the expression on your face. After discovering your own likes and dislikes, comforts and discomforts in movement, you will explore new possibilities in motion and discover many new likes and meanings, extend the range of what is comfortable for you, so that the possibilities for your choreography become greater.

Learning Experience

Compare yourself with a close friend. How are you physically, emotionally, intellectually, and socially different and alike? Observe your friend's movement. How do you differ in this respect? How are you similar? Can you identify any characteristics about your friend that seem to influence his or her movements? About yourself?

---

4. Dance enables you to explore and understand space, time, and energy.

The elements of dance have to do with the way energy is expended and the way time and space are used. You are always influenced by these abstract elements in everyday living, although you may not be consciously aware of it and of your reaction to it.

You have feelings about space and about yourself in space. You may feel cozy in a corner, or like to sit close to other people; or you may feel comfortable all curled up, in a place that is particularly yours. You may like lots of room, or like to experience different places in a room; you may feel hampered by crowds and penned up in subways. You may go in a single direction, or you may like to wander, trying many new paths. Some people constantly go around in circles.

You are sensitive to things outside yourself in space. You may be thrilled by the height of a skyscraper jutting into the sky, or you may like the soft curves of rolling hills. You may laugh at squat, round shapes, or be threatened by square corners. You may feel that angles are exciting, or that off-balances are intriguing. You will make use of these sensitivities and awarenesses in your dances, and perhaps in your use of the stage.

Then, too, you will develop responses to other people's use of space. You may react in a certain way to people who seem absolutely open and unprotected, and in another way to people who keep their arms and legs tightly crossed, tapping only one finger. You know each of them from the way they are in space.

In dance, you will have new spatial experiences. You will try to simulate curves in all parts of your body, make your legs appear longer, your knees round. You will condense space and expand it, perhaps break it up, but never ignore it.

Time is another element with which you are concerned daily — by watch, bell, or bus schedule. It makes you hurry, allows you to be lazy, or may cause anxiety. Time is continuous; it goes on regardless of what you do. You can go with it or against it; you can get caught up in the hurry or drift along slowly. You may know yourself as one who enjoys running with your motor revved up, making sudden starts and stops, and being excited by an unexpected change. On the other hand, you may be one who likes slowness, who is secure in the expected, and is lulled by routine.

You know time already, and will know it better as you progress in dance. You will discover new slowness and fastness, the effect of continuity and of contrast, and the sense of time passing. You will become aware of the rhythm of breathing, of feeling, and of motion. You will move in, with, and through time, and you will use it in brand new ways.

Dance uses energy carefully and meaningfully. You do this every day — you use energy to accomplish what you set out to do. You know yourself in relation to energy, as well as in time and space. There are times when you abound in it, being explosive and volatile; other times you have little energy, being tired and droopy. Perhaps you just use it carefully, in light and delicate ways. Your energy may be contained and ready for important things, always there just below the surface, popping into your eyes in a ready smile, making your mouth corners turn up, or perhaps turn down in a sudden outburst of temper. Your energy may always be channeled into tension, existing as an unquestioned habit, like drinking coffee and smoking cigarettes. What you sense as energy has a lot to do with what we call *personality*.

Energy is closely linked with time and space. Energy is necessary for one to move through space, and moving through space takes time. Each element is affected by all the others. If you must hurry to go somewhere far away, tension accumulates. If you have lots of time and nowhere to go, energy may be held in reserve.

Energy is carefully defined in dance. Movement can be accomplished only by its expenditure, and will be qualified by the way in which it is expended. It can be dissected into vibrations per second, exploded in short sharp bursts, or used to help you resist the temptation to give in and collapse. You will know energy, how to generate it, and how and where to spend it. Movement will require it; the idea will require it; your energy will command them both.

Movement in dance, then, will include articulation of all these elements at once, in the same way that they always exist simultaneously. Space, time, and energy are your raw materials. They are what dance is about.

Learning Experience

Does all movement involve energy, time, and space? As you move in your daily life, concentrate on each of these aspects one at a time, trying to become more aware of them. Watch for them in the movement of others.

---

5. **Dance training includes experiences in technique, moving through space, improvisation, choreography, and performance.**

In your encounter with dance, each experience will be a new one. Even if you were presented with the same motional problem a thousand times, you would find a thousand different ways to solve it. The reasons are, of course, that the possibilities for human movement are nearly limitless, and you are never the same person you were when you solved the problem the first time or the second or the twenty-seventh.

Your experiences in dance education will probably fall into five general areas: technique, moving through space, improvisation, choreography, and performance. You will not necessarily work with them in that order, as they are not sequentially related. You may work in all five areas in a single day's class. The experiences in this book have been chosen to give you a variety of new sensations in motion and a number of different approaches to your own creative resources. Since these experiences will not necessarily happen chronologically, this book does not recommend a particular order of events. You may prefer to skip around and read what is pertinent to you at each stage of your own development.

Most dance classes begin with *technique,* the purpose of which is to develop awareness of and fully articulate your body selves. Through the practice of daily rituals, you stretch, strengthen, and coordinate yourselves toward the goal of versatility — being able to move in any way you like. Classes designed to develop your technique might include warm-up exercises, combinations of discrete movements, or sequences of movements through space. The goal is to be able to perform specific movements in a specific way. Thus, ballet technique emphasizes developing the capability to perform complex ballet movements. Modern dance pioneers such as Graham and Humphrey had to develop their own techniques in order to train other dancers to be able to perform their compositions. In this way, distinct "techniques" developed to achieve highly personal movement goals.

Technique may continue or develop through a period of moving through space, quite a different sensation from moving in one place. Often this will consist of a movement combination presented by your instructor as a means for you to work on some particular principle of motion. The combination, in itself, is not the important thing; the point of view *is.* It is just like algebra: once you understand the principle, you can solve any problem.

Improvisation has nothing to do with imitating movement patterns or learning combinations for their own sake. You will spend much of your time discovering movement and creating patterns for yourself. This is the greatest fun of all, as there is unlimited material from which to draw. In this book you will find experiences in which you are asked to *explore* a particular area of movement. By this, it is meant that you should try many solutions to the problem, stopping, starting, going back, and trying another. It is an exhaustive type of search, narrowly focused within certain limitations. When you *improvise*, you move spontaneously, letting one movement lead into the next. You try not to stop or break the flow of movement associations. You may start out searching for a specific kind of movement, but may discover that the search has led you to something far more interesting. You keep right on going, wherever the improvisation leads you. Improvisation is less strictly channeled than exploration, and is continuous in time from beginning to end.

From your experiences in motion you will *choreograph* your own studies and dances. You will find movement or idea materials through the processes of exploration and improvisation in the same way that you discover new ideas through occasional spontaneous, unplanned, or uncalculated responses. You will shape these discovered materials into some final form as a dance in the same way that you order your thoughts in certain organizations. While these kinds of thoughts are concerned with words, dance is concerned with motion, or with particular sensed thoughts or feelings that are as yet beyond words, or nonverbal. In dance you will organize shapes, rhythms, dynamics, and movement ideas.

You organize your thoughts in order to communicate them to others by writing or speaking them. You will be forming movement for the same ultimate purpose — for sharing the form with others. After all, even though it may be very satisfying simply to have a new idea or a fresh solution to a problem, the maximum pleasure comes in telling someone else about it. When your dance is exciting and meaningful to you, you will want others to see it. Your dances will not be large-scale epics at this stage of the game, but they will afford you additional opportunities to solidify your movement experience.

You will *perform*. You will perform for and with your class, for your instructor, for friends, and for strangers. You will perform not only choreographies, but every small part of every exercise, of every step across the floor, and of every improvisation. Performance is not just "dancing the dance." It is being present and being supremely aware in each motion and moment. Performance sounds a little frightening, perhaps, but when you consider that you present yourself to many people in many situations every day, it is a quite natural occurrence. It is spine-tingling because it occurs in that coveted and, at the same time, fearsome center of attention. It will be most meaningful as an experience if you have something of value to offer while you are there. The book has this end in mind.

Learning Experience

Attend a modern dance performance. Upon reflection, can you separate the aspect of technique from that of choreography from that of performance? Can you see how the synthesis of these, perfect or imperfect, contributes to or detracts from the entire presentation?

3

The Body Instrument

CONCEPT: *The body instrument requires intelligent, sensitive cultivation and tuning for dance.*

The tool of the violinist is the instrument, of the painter the brush, of the dancer the body. As dancer, you *are* the instrument, so treat yourself with intelligence, sensitivity, and kindness as well as practicing discipline and total awareness. You will live both inside and outside yourself so as to see as well as feel what is going on. A good way to practice this being in two places at once is to watch yourself breathing. It is something we are always doing but seldom pay attention to.

1. The breath is the primal act, that which vitalizes and sensitizes all of us, all parts of us.

It is no accident that to breathe in is called inspiration — that which brings us to life. The first and last act of a lifetime is that of breathing. To take our first breath is to establish separation from the mother and to let go of the last one is to return home again. In between these two significant events, breathing is the harmonizing of actions, going on continually without our conscious control, responding naturally to our feelings and needs. How reassuring that this life-sustaining act goes on all by itself without our having to direct or control it. It incorporates opening and closing, lifting and lowering, filling and emptying, taking in and giving out, all in perfect balance. To pay attention to our breathing allows us to focus on this natural balance, centers and calms us, and is a wonderful place to begin the dance.

Learning Experience

Lying on your back on the floor, allow your natural breathing to go on its own way, feeling and watching it come and go. Feel the expanding and contracting of the rib cage and visualize the swelling and emptying of the lungs. Allow yourself to move as an extension of that breathing action. What shape does that movement take? Feel it and see it.

Concentrate on the inhalation, sending breath to various body parts, lightening and energizing them. Feel parts of you floating like helium balloons. Then focus on the exhalation, giving in to the weight of each part, giving in to relaxation.

Breath can be used to energize and to relax. Coordinating breathing with moving enlivens and enriches the quality of the motion. In the experiences that follow, find a way to breathe with them for the fullest and most satisfying feeling.

2. An understanding of the body parts and their movement potential makes more intelligent movement possible.

You will experience your body as a whole and also in its separate parts. You know your nose from your toes, and have since earliest childhood, so a discussion of the parts of the body may seem superfluous. In dance, however, there are certain parts that need specific attention. These need to be clarified, so that you will speak not of the back, but of the lower, middle, or upper spine, and not of the hip bone when you really mean the hip joint.

The spine is basic to all human movement. It is a long series of bones extending from the base of the head, at about ear level, to the *coccyx*, or tailbone. It consists of 24 separate bones, or *vertebrae*, and two others, the *sacrum* and *coccyx*.

The spine has natural curves in it — a forward curve at the neck, a backward curve at the ribs, another forward curve at the waist, and a backward curve below the waist. These curves are meant to be there, but are not meant to be exaggerated. Fluidity of motion in the spine is a desirable asset to the dancer, and many of the things you will be asked to do are designed to give more mobility to the spine by working the curves opposite to their normal direction.

For convenience, you can speak of the spine in three sections. The *upper spine* extends from the base of the head to just below the shoulder blades. The *middle spine* continues from there to waist level, and the *lower spine* includes the remaining vertebrae, the sacrum, and the coccyx. Each of these areas can be trained to operate independently of the others, or together as a totality.

Learning Experience

Locate the 3 spinal areas on a friend or in yourself with your side to a mirror. Breathe into the upper spine while rounding it forward. Now deepen the curve by rounding the middle spine; now bend forward from the hip joint and breathe into the whole length of the spine and any place in the back or legs that feels tight.

Rounding in 3 areas of the spine.

The area of the hips is often a confusing one. The *hip bones*, first of all, are the prominent bones found on the front of the body, about three inches below the waist and about shoulder width apart. The *hip joint* is where the leg is attached to the torso.

Learning Experience

Put the heel of your hand on your hip bone and extend your fingers downward. Your palm will cross your hip joint. Lift your thigh forward and feel the break in your hip joint.

Later, when you read "hips forward," this is the part of your hip that is directed forward — the whole area you just covered with your hand. The *side of your hips* is at the same level as your hip joint and can be felt as prominent bones on the sides of your body.

Learning Experience

Place your thumb at your waist and stretch your middle finger down the side of your body. It will reach the area known as the side of the hip. Let your weight sink into one hip, and you will easily find this area.

Further on, when you read of moving your hips in a backward direction, this means that the whole lower spine area is moving backward, not just the tip of your spine. Moving only the tip of your spine will cause your pelvis to tilt, exaggerating the curve at your waist in the well-known "swayback" posture; this is to be avoided in most cases.

One other important body part is the *sternum*, or breastbone. This is, for the dancer, the focal point of the chest and a key to much of the dancer's movement. A lifted sternum may exude confidence or haughtiness; a sunken sternum might suggest timidity, fatigue, or perhaps softness. The sternum is also important in balance. Its placement over the ball of the foot means stability when standing, moving, or balancing on it.

Learning Experience

Practice lifting the sternum and letting it sink. Observe the effect of this on the whole spine. Note the resultant feeling in your muscles and joints.

The rest of the body terminology used in dance is much the same as you have learned from childhood.

(In many of the following experiences, you will be asked to improvise and choreograph. You might find it helpful to read Chapters 4 and 5 now, and again later as you progress. Understanding more and more about improvisation and choreography will make your experiences with them that much richer. Conversely, the more experiences you have in these areas, the greater will be your understanding of the material in this book.)

Learning Experiences

Explore the parts of your body individually. Choose a hand, shoulder, head, hip, or any other part. Discover what its possibilities for movement are, then use it to initiate movement of your whole body. Move several parts in a sequence. Move one part while moving another in the same way, then in a contrasting way.

Improvise with body parts, projecting each particular part more strongly than you project the total body. By your own attention to them, make the viewer see just your head, your knee, or your elbow.

Explore the possibilities for movement with two parts of the body connected: an elbow to a knee, a hand to a foot, or both hands joined behind the neck. Try the same problem with another person, moving head to head, hand to foot, back to back, or shoulder to hip.

Improvise with one or more people, relating your movement to theirs. Choose the same body parts or different ones. Find that delicate balance of movement relationship in which you are subtly influenced by each other's motion, without either of you imitating or dominating the other.

3. The action possible for each joint determines the movement available for dance.

Before reading about the body in motion, focus for a minute on the joints, which give you the possibility of motion. Different joints are capable of different actions. There are a few terms you should know in order to facilitate the discussion of joint actions.

Some joints allow only two actions. They either *flex* (bend) or *extend* (straighten). An example of this is the knee. Other joints, such as the hip joint, flex and extend too, but they have other actions as well. All of the appendages (legs, arms, head) can *rotate* at the point where they join the torso. A rotary action is one in which the body part holds its own place in space, but twists around itself. In other words, it rotates around its own axis. The arm can rotate in the shoulder joint, the leg in the hip joint, and the head on top of the spine.

Circumduction is an action that occurs when one end of a body part is fixed at its attachment and the other traces a circular path in space. An example of this action is a swing of the arm from the shoulder joint. The circle need not be complete.

Learning Experience

By yourself, improvise with your concentration on the joints and their actions, rather than on the body parts which meet at these joints. Explore the range and type of each joint's movement. Allow your total body to participate but, through your skill, draw the attention to the selected joint you are exploring. Experiment with new placements of joints in space. Arrange a sequence of joint actions, projecting each new joint in its turn.

---

4. Movement experiences with body parts develop more sensitive articulation for the dance.

The *torso* is the center of your physical control. It is the trunk from which the movements of your limbs originate. The torso — spine, hips, shoulders, that which encloses the apparatus of the heart, lungs, and the vital organs of life — is quite naturally the center of movement and feelings.

Learning Experience

Sitting crosslegged on the floor, lengthen your spine, elongate the back of your neck and your lower back. Open your upper back and let the ribs drop. Let the arms hang easily at the shoulders and think of a small waist. Now breathe easily in this position and see how balanced it feels. Move away from this position and note the resulting tensions, the need for adjustment in the whole torso, and possibly even in the arms and legs.

The *upper torso* is an important area, as it affects breathing, the use of the arms, and the uplifted appearance of the whole body. It is, however, one of the areas of least mobility because of the rib cage residing there. It is necessary to work conscientiously to accomplish the subtle articulations possible to this area.

Arching over by squeezing ribs and by lifting them.

Learning Experiences

Lift and carry your rib cage straight across to the right, through center, over to the left, and through center again. Press it forward, come center, press out through your upper back, then return. (Keep your hips stationary, with the shoulders maintaining a horizontal line.) Circle the upper torso, carrying the rib cage from right to forward to left and back, around a vertical axis, in a horizontal plane.

Arch your body to the side by squeezing your right ribs together. Now arch to the same side by lifting your ribs, pressing up with your left side, leaving no wrinkles in your leotard. Check yourself in a mirror to see the different line, as well as the different feeling, of these two actions.

If the *head* is used as an extension of the action of the upper torso, the result is one of harmony in the body parts. If you carry your head rigidly, or in a direction opposite the body lean, you will feel a contrast of pulls and a sense of conflict. Be aware of the effects on the body and the feelings resulting from different uses of the head.

The *lower torso* is of equal and perhaps greater importance, for here is located your true center of gravity and the control for your legs, both in gesture and in weight-bearing functions. You should know what movement is possible in the lower torso, and how to control this area while others are moving so that balance is maintained.

Learning Experiences

With your shoulders and rib cage still, slide the hips from side to side. Press gently forward through your hip joints, then pull back through your lower back. Come to a centered position again. Holding all else still, circle your hips around a vertical axis, keeping your hip bones parallel to the floor.

Now, allowing your ribs and shoulders to participate, send your hips to the right and let your rib cage drop to the left. Again send your hips to the right, but this time lift your rib cage up and away from your right hip, arching up and over to the left. Feel the difference.

In a standing position, twist your hips to the left, resisting at first through your ribs, then letting your ribs follow, then your shoulder and even your arm. Then twist your hips back to the right, letting the rest of your torso follow sequentially.

There are a great many movements possible to the peripheral parts of the body: to the head, the arms, and the legs. It is possible to move all these parts in isolation, or the motivation for the movement of the periphery can come from the center, making the statement with the total body. Either one is a legitimate use of the body, and each will probably find its place in your choreography.

The *arms* have many possibilities for action: lifting and lowering (forward and back and to the side), rotation and circumduction at the shoulder joint, not to

Arm lift involving shoulder blades. See how this feels.

mention the endless possibilities of variation when one adds actions of elbow and wrist joints. But it is not the "whats" that each joint can do, but "how" they can do them that make dance fascinating.

Learning Experiences

Start to lift your arms by pulling down on the muscles below your shoulder blades. Once your arms are at the horizontal, pull down even harder. Feel the deep connections of your arm muscles with your back.

Now lift your arms with as little torso participation as possible. Feel the difference between these two experiences.

Lift your right arm to the side, letting your hand begin the action. Now try the same action beginning with your elbow — and now with your shoulder. Finally, let your arm rise as a result of the sequential pressing to the side of your hip, rib cage, and shoulder. Your arm rises as the result of the sideward unfolding of your whole body.

The arms have a natural tendency to reflect the movement of the rest of the body, and you will capitalize on this tendency much of the time. You may also find it of interest to try resisting this natural impulse.

Learning Experience

Take a high lift in your torso up and over to the right, pulling your left arm down hard against it. Do the same action again, but continue the upward line of your spine with your arm. Note the difference in sensations.

Since there are two of them, your arms can become quite complicated in their patterns. They can move in unison with each other and with the torso, or opposite, not only to each other and to the torso, but to the legs and head. Arm movement can be purely decorative — separate from the body — or organically related to movement originating in the torso.

Learning Experience

Try lifting one arm forward while the other bends at your elbow joint across in front of your body. Meanwhile, twist your torso slightly to the left. Feel the result.

Hands can be the most magical and articulate part of you. Sometimes this is to their detriment rather than their favor. There is so much movement possible for them that they often do things which distract from the real point of the movement, or which are inconsistent with its total quality. Imagine the little finger elegantly crooked, in the midst of strong angular motions of the arms and legs. This sometimes can happen without your slightest awareness. You should explore the possibilities for movement in your hands, not only to know what is available for use, but also to develop an awareness of them and so make them consciously a part of your moving body.

Learning Experiences

Curl your fingers into your palm and open them out. As you curl your fingers, turn your palm down; as you open out, turn your palm up. With your open hand, spread your fingers wide apart and draw them back together; do this same thing with your arms extended forward at shoulder level, palms facing forward.

Now, to feel your fingers as extensions of your body, throw your right arm forward, allowing your fingers to open at the end of the throw. Feel the energy start from your shoulder and continue out through your fingertips. Find the right response for your hands in all other arm movements experienced so far.

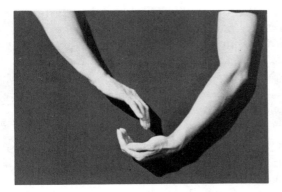

Hands have texture,
emphasize shape or motion.

Your *legs*, as well as your arms, lift and lower, rotate and circumduct. Their movement, however, differs from that of the arms in that their function is double. They are attached at the hip joint, so there is movement possible from there. They are also temporarily attached at the other end to the floor, responsible for supporting your weight or carrying it through space. There are times when their motional possibilities are more limited by this added responsibility than are those of the arms. Yet, the unique possibilities inherent in this limitation are quite fascinating.

Learning Experience

While standing, bend both knees, one pointed forward, the other pointed in, then pointed out. (Your foot on this side bears weight only on the ball.) In accomplishing this rotation of your thigh, feel the difference between allowing your leg to swing back and forth by its own weight, and turning outward by a tightening of the outward rotators deep in the side of your hip. Now rotate both thighs out and straighten your knees.

While you are in this last position, consider that this "turned-out" position of your hip joint is used a great deal in dance. This is so for a number of good reasons. Among them is the fact that the leg articulates more freely in the hip joint and bears weight more securely in that position. Travel to the side is much more easily done, and the sculptural lines of the body may be enhanced by the outward rotation of the legs.

The legs, even when not bearing weight, can still use their contact with the floor to good advantage. In a leg swing, as the leg brushes forward, the foot stays in contact with the floor until its arc lifts it up into space. The energy that was first used to push along the floor is then used to lift the leg. In a hop or jump, the height of the elevation comes not only from the extension of the leg joints, but also from the energy used in pressing away from the floor. If the legs are used to make a quick gesture in the air, the movement must of course be sharp, as the moment of suspension is brief, but also very exciting.

Legs design and gesture.

Learning Experience

Lying on the floor, explore the combinations of flexion and extension of all your leg joints. Experiment with rotation and circumduction at your hip joint. Find new ways to support yourself while you discover new ways to use your legs.

Feet could be as articulate and mobile as hands. Unfortunately, they are usually used as solid blocks of support packed up tight in shoes. Consequently they lose a good deal of their flexibility and facility. Too often you consider them only as beasts of burden; however, as you sit and relieve them of their load, you may explore what they can do.

Learning Experience

Curl and uncurl your toes; spread them apart; relax. Press down through your arches, then draw them up. Turn the soles of your feet toward each other, then away. Crawl up one leg with the toes of your other foot. Flex and extend your ankles in unison, then in sequence. Do different things with each foot at the same time. Explore all the possibilities, not only sitting, but lying down and standing.

The working of your legs is complicated by their double function of support and gesture. Much of their action is determined by the requirements of balance

Legs also support weight in different ways.

in a particular movement. Though they are attached to the hips and move by virtue of muscles originating there, they usually move independently of the hips. They move while the torso holds its stability. Lifting a leg will seldom be preceded by lifting a hip unless the choreography calls for it.

While awareness of each individual part of your body is important, even more important is your awareness of your *total body*, of the relationship of parts both at rest and in motion. Here, there is interaction and integration, which can produce a symphony of movement as well as a solo for one part.

Learning Experience

Just as you improvised projecting awareness of single body parts, now improvise projecting your entire body. Make the viewer aware of your total body, rather than of any single part.

---

5. The parts of the body work together in a particular way for a particular effect.

So much for the separate parts of your body. As has been suggested throughout this section, the important thing is that all the parts are interconnected and interrelated. Movement of one part implies motional tendencies of the other parts. When the torso moves, for example, there seems to be a natural tendency for the arms, legs, and head to accompany this motion in a particular way. If you wish to produce harmony, you allow these tendencies to be fully realized. If you wish to connote disharmony, you deny the natural complementary movement. Isolating and using single parts of the body in illogical order can have a humorous effect, or produce the illusion of the body being controlled from the outside.

6. Physical laws affecting the body in motion determine limitations and potential for dance.

As well as enjoying the motion and energy of your own body, you'll be interested in the forces of the universe that act upon you. You will explore relating to, controlling, and using these forces, and become aware of how these forces affect and even control you. As they are constant and consistently operating, your dealing with them is important. You will use your body with or against these forces in overcoming inertia, resisting the pull of gravity, controlling momentum, using centripetal and centrifugal force in order to control and execute balances, falls, turns, and circles, to go easily from starts to stops to starts again, and to change direction with clarity and control. These forces are present and real, and relating to them in a particular way has meaning inherent in it. You can choose to use them and relate to them in unorthodox ways. There are countless ways of going from a state of inertia into motion. You may dance in defiance of gravity, give in to it, or build patterns of both in space.

Gravity affects dance in balances, falls, and elevations. You relate specifically to gravity in everything that you do. You hold your body up against the downward pull of it, in most cases. You rise above it in precarious balances, and give in to it in falls.

When dancing, it is essential to *maintain your natural height in relation to the downward pull of gravity.* Proper alignment, which refers to the correct relationship of your body parts to each other and to gravity, makes it possible for you to do this. Staying in an easy lifted position, your length is emphasized; therefore, the spine is elongated and its curves minimized. In this state, you stand easily with a minimum of effort. If one part is out of alignment, all parts are off and a lot more energy is required to hold yourself upright.

Learning Experience

To experience "good alignment," ground yourself: stand evenly on both feet. Then, feel the back of the neck as an extension of the tailbone; line up a point right behind the ear with the center of the shoulder, over the center of the hip, over a point on the foot just ahead of the ankle. Close your eyes and get a good taste of what that position feels like.

To avoid confusion in thinking of the body in terms of its separate parts, pulling in here and pushing out there, think of only two things when taking this standing position. One is the lengthening of the spine from the middle of the back down through the tailbone, and up through the top of the head. The other is relaxing everything else not involved in this lengthening — the shoulders, the arms, the ribs, the buttocks, and even the face. The result should be a feeling of lift, of compactness, of being "on top of yourself" without undue strain or tension. While here, breathe energy up from the earth through your feet, energize your full length with it, and exhale it heavenward through the top of your head.

So far, we have described a front/back alignment, most visible from the side of the dancer. There is also right/left balance. If that is out of whack, weight is not evenly balanced on both feet. The spine may be snaking across the back instead of going right through the center, causing a higher hip and opposite shoulder. This is the frontal aspect of alignment, visible from the front or back. Then there is, on the horizontal plane, a sense that you are firmly settled down on the floor but lengthening upwards at the same time: rooted in the earth but with energy streaming upward through the trunk and making tingly sensations through the neck and out of the top of the head.

Right / left balance.

Front / back alignment.

When your right/left, front/back, top/bottom dimensions are in balance, you will have a great sense of well-being. While here in this positive place of beginnings, you can sense the point at which all three of these dimensions meet. Identify this as your *center*: the point at which the energy churns, from which energy generates out in all directions. This point, called the *center of gravity*, is actually, physically, about an inch below the belly button, although it is higher on broad-chested, wide-shouldered persons and lower on full-hipped people. From a psychic perspective, you may find your center of energy in a variety of other places: some dancers have felt centered from the solar plexis, while others speak of moving from the heart.

Alignment sounds like a pretty static proposition. It is a good place to begin from and return to. When the center is identified, you move from that center, keeping that center over the base of support so that balance is maintained, though sometimes greatly challenged. When you balance on one foot, the center of gravity moves over the ball of that foot, or when you rise to the ball of the foot, the center shifts forward and lifts also. Balance is something each person must discover individually. When you achieve it, note the muscular feel at that moment, the relative placement of each part of the body, and remember it. Try to achieve that same alignment many times until it becomes a habit.

When you go from standing still into movement — movement of one part or movement of the whole body through space — your alignment shifts to accommodate that movement. Sometimes it shifts just a little to support lifting the arms or swinging one leg; other times it shifts a lot to accomplish spiral falls or curving turns; and other times, it simply goes with you through space, as you run, skip, leap, and land, preparing new bases of support to allow you to land and take off again. Different choreographers deal with gravity in various ways. These differences are all a matter of choreographic style, adjustments of alignment to project the specific artistic taste of the choreographer. The laws of science in counterbalance with the requirements of art, the cosmic energies interacting with human energies, make dance a continually exciting and dynamic event.

Another law of physics relating to balance is the familiar one of *action and reaction*. For every action, there is an equal and opposite reaction. If, in your standing alignment, one part is out of the vertical line, there must be a compensatory shift out of line in the opposite direction by another part. If you lift a leg behind you, another part of you will be displaced in a forward direction in order to keep from falling — perhaps your chest or your arms — or you might shift your whole body slightly forward from the ankle.

Learning Experiences

Practice balancing on one foot. Place your chest over the ball of your foot and extend your ankle. If you fall forward, readjust. If you fall backward, compensate by moving your chest slightly forward. Find your own point of balance. Then consciously shift the position of your body and discover what sort of compensatory action is necessary for balance to be maintained. With one foot flat on the floor, work in different positions of your torso, twisting and bending, even to a position parallel with the floor. Find out how much movement is possible in this balanced position.

Improvise with another person, both of you working in positions of precarious balance, using each other for assistance. Realize the tremendous sensitivity and care necessary in maintaining this double balance.

Challenging balance alone.

Challenging balance with another.

Sometimes it is desirable to *give in to gravity*. Diving, dropping, falling, and collapsing movements are important in the vocabulary of the dancer for changing levels of space and for the quality of motion which results from the withdrawal of energy. As with other kinds of motion, you can practice in it with the total body or with a single body part. You might withdraw the energy from a raised arm in short successive drops, or you might choose to fall flat on the floor.

In falling, you will discover that a progression of parts rolling onto the floor in sequence will dissipate the force of the fall and save you from bruised knees and elbows. Counterbalance your weight as you go down, so that all the weight is not going into one part of the body near the floor, but so that some of it is held in the opposite, balancing part. You will learn, hopefully not the hard way, that you should land on the padded parts of the body — not on the bony, jointed corners. From down, you will discover the way back up. Control the going down and up in the stronger areas of the body: the thighs, back, and abdomen.

Learning Experience

Explore the possibilities of falling, with various parts of your body starting first — your hip, your knee, your shoulder, your head, and your hand. Since you have to get up to explore the next way down, try different possibilities of rising from the floor.

A third way of using gravity is to *resist* it — to push away from the floor in hops, leaps, and jumps. These adventures into open space are collectively called *elevations*. In order to elevate successfully, you must use more force in pushing yourself up than gravity uses in pulling you down. A good deep knee bend *(plié)* as preparation, followed by a swift extension of all the leg joints *(relevé)*, will launch you. Applying the "action-reaction" principle again, the farther down the knee bend takes you (within reason), the higher you should rise into the air.

Pliés and relevés, in addition to being important exercises for building leg strength, are the actions you do when taking off and landing from elevations. The plié is the preparatory flexion of the legs which gives you the power to rise, as well as the cushion which absorbs your weight as you land. The relevé is the forceful extension of the legs which sends you into the air, and the prelude to the landing plié which eases you back to the floor. The names for these actions are borrowed from French ballet, as are the movements themselves. But they are so integral a part of all dance that no one discipline can claim them as its exclusive property.

Learning Experiences

To practice the plié, begin with your body in good alignment and your legs turned out at your hip joint. As your legs bend, direct your knees out over the center of your feet. For a demi-plié *(small), flex your legs only until your heels want to lift from the floor. At this point, return to the starting position by straightening your knees, keeping them turned out all the while. For a* grande plié *(large), continue your knee bend down past the point where your heels lift from the floor to where your hips are just elevated from your heels and the weight is still carried in your thighs. The return occurs by placing your heels down as your body lifts and then extending your knees. In both pliés, your spine maintains its length and alignment and your pelvis tips neither forward nor back.*

To practice the relevé, stand again in good alignment with your legs turned out at your hip joint, and slowly extend your hips, knees, and ankles to their maximum, so that your body rises on the balls of your feet. Then, keeping your knees straight, lower your heels to the floor, opposing this downward action with a feeling of lifting through your chest at the same time.

You will no doubt practice pliés and relevés a great deal in the course of your class. They are highly important exercises in themselves, as well as vital to elevations. They build strength in the hips and legs and provide continual opportunity to practice good alignment. They are the means by which the body changes level and travels upward and downward. So important are they that the dancer performs them repeatedly, almost like ritual prayer, as a part of daily training.

The body may do all kinds of things once it is in the air, but it should be in proper alignment when taking off or it may be misdirected in the air. Once you are in the air in an elevation, you have no balance problem. As you require no support, you do not have to worry about it — that is, until you have to land. Before landing, prepare a base of support (a foot or feet), and see that your center of gravity is placed over it.

Learning Experience

Practice jumping in all directions, including turning. Jump with your legs in various relationships in the air. Jump with your body making different shapes in the air.

Jumps in many shapes.

Centrifugal and centripetal forces affect a body in circular motion. Another physical law that you will encounter when performing turns and circles is the one involving centrifugal and centripetal forces. You have experienced centrifugal force when, as a child, you stood in one spot and whirled around with your arms out wide and felt the tingling sensation of blood rushing to your hands. *Centrifugal force* is that which tends to impel a thing toward the outside of a center of rotation. This is counterbalanced by *centripetal force,* which pulls inward toward the center of rotation. You may have experienced this force as a child, too, when you rounded the corner on your bicycle and leaned inward to make the turn. If you leaned in too far, you fell off and became painfully aware of the dangers of unbalanced centripetal and centrifugal forces.

When you move through space in a curved path, you will find that these forces work upon you just as they do upon any circling body. You will find yourself molding your body to the shape of the curve, leaning inward with part of your body to counteract the outward force of the turn. The faster you go, the stronger the effect of these forces. It is the "hows" you discover to balance these forces that make turning and circling so interesting and exciting. There is always one more way to turn.

In *turning*, you revolve around an imaginary axis that runs vertically somewhere through your body. It may go from your head through a point between your feet, if you are upright and turning on both feet. Or, if you are doing a tilted turn on one foot, the theoretical axis may go through one shoulder down through the ball of the foot. You may even turn and travel through space at the same time, taking the imaginary axis with you. However you turn, it is the quality of the turn that you want to bring out in your performance. It is the continuity of the revolution that gives turning its character as a motion.

Circling, as opposed to turning, involves moving through space around an imaginary vertical axis which lies outside the body. More simply, it is moving on the outside edge of a circle. You will feel your relationship to that circle's imaginary center and discover what adjustments you must make to centrifugal and centripetal force to keep moving in that circular path. Again, it is the quality of the curve that is to be brought out in your performance.

You can also move in curved paths in a vertical plane. These vertical curves are often referred to as *overcurves* and *undercurves*. As their names imply, the overcurve describes the top half of a circle, and the undercurve describes the bottom half.

Overcurves and undercurves rely heavily on the use of the plié and relevé. An undercurve can begin in relevé, but usually begins in normal standing position. Try one.

Learning Experience

With the weight on your right foot, plié, lowering the weight of your body. Transfer your weight forward in plié to your left leg, and straighten it. The undercurve has been accomplished.

You may perform an undercurve with the whole body or with one part. A leg swing is an undercurve. The on-the-ground phase of the skip is also an undercurve.

An overcurve usually begins in plié, particularly since it often involves air moments, for which a preparation for take-off and a cushioned landing are essential.

Learning Experience

Your weight is on your right leg and the path of travel is up and forward. Straighten your leg to relevé. Transfer your weight forward to your left foot in relevé. Lower your weight by performing a plié on your left leg. Try it now with a push-off, so that an air moment occurs during the transfer of weight from one foot to the other.

An overcurve is the path the body follows in a leap, jump, or any elevation that travels through space.

Learning Experiences

Improvise movements entirely in curved paths. Let all your gestures be rounded. Let your feet trace only curved paths on the floor, and let your body always shape to the arc of the movement.

Improvise with a group, wherein only one person is self-starting. The others can begin motion only when a moving body comes near them. The paths of motion are always orbital, or circular, and can change only when made to do so by the passing or colliding force of another body. Try to let your body react as a freely moving object in space, without imposing your will upon its motion.

Inertia and momentum must be considered in designing "going" and "stopping" in dance. Finally, you will be concerned with overcoming *inertia*, with the gathering up of energy to move from a static position. This can take the form of a *gesture*, in which one part of the body moves through space, or the form of *locomotion*, in which the whole body moves through space and across space. In either case, energy must be expended to make the initial move. Once the action is begun, its momentum will carry it along until the motivating energy runs out or until more energy is summoned to halt the momentum.

Gestures, such as arm swings, leg swings, and head nods, are performed in one place and need no extra consideration, unless performed with such extreme force that the body is sent off balance or off through space. Sometimes this is done intentionally, with the rest of the body following sequentially, and still under control. At other times, it is as though this part of the body were possessed of another spirit. For the most part, gestures are isolated actions, with the torso holding upright or molding to be in consonance with the gesture. Gestures of two parts at once — such as leg and arm swings — are usually performed in opposition to maintain balance.

In locomotion, however, there are several additional considerations. When the whole body begins to move through space, there must first be a weight shift in the direction of travel in order to overcome inertia. In order to take a step forward, for example, there is a shift of weight into a forward direction and then a receiving of it on a new base of support — the other foot. The timing of the weight shift and the placing of the new base is variable, but in normal walking they occur in sequence: the weight begins to shift forward, a new base is formed to receive it, and the weight arrives over the new base of support.

Conversely, when one wants to stop, *momentum* must be overcome. The weight, which has been displaced in the direction travelled, must be brought back over the base of support.

Learning Experience

Run at full speed and stop suddenly. Notice how your weight shifts backward before you stop. Now try to stop without this weight shift. Be careful.

Locomotion is usually defined as movement through space, carrying the weight from one base of support to another. As in the above, the bases of support are usually thought of as the feet, but there are many other possibilities. All the other parts of the body can be used in combination.

Learning Experiences

Explore ways of going through space on your back, on your side, and on your stomach. Use your feet and hands for pulling and pushing. Try locomotion on anything but your feet.

Find locomotions involving transfer of your weight to different bases of support. You may use your feet as well as anything else that will hold you. Use four supports, then try two, then one. Vary these by changing the direction that you are facing. Face the floor, the ceiling, and then the wall as you travel.

Locomotion using the hips as support.

The conventional and generally accepted basic methods of locomotion on foot are as follows:

1. *Walk:* the simplest kind of locomotion. A walk is a transfer of weight from one foot to the other.
2. *Run:* an extension of the walk. A run is also a transfer of weight from one foot to the other, but the stride is longer and the speed of travel faster. There is a brief moment in which neither foot is in contact with the floor.
3. *Leap:* a further extension of the run. A leap also goes from one foot to the other, but the distance covered is even greater than in the run, and the air moment is longer.

Fully extended leap.

4. *Hop:* a transfer of weight from one foot back to the same foot. The take-off and landing foot are the same, and there is necessarily a moment of elevation.
5. *Jump:* a landing on two feet after a take-off from one or both feet. The body is airborne at one moment during the jump.

Airborne in a jump.

There are also the following well-known combinations, each having its own distinctive rhythmic pattern.

6. *Skip:* a combination of a walk (or step) and hop, in a slow-quick rhythm.
7. *Gallop:* a combination of a step and leap, moving forward, in quick-slow time.
8. *Slide:* a combination of step and leap, moving sidewards, like the gallop in rhythm.

Learning Experiences

Improvise on the simplest of these locomotions, the walk. Walk heel first, then toe first, turned in, turned out, and both fast and slow. Try many different uses of your feet and legs.

Devise a number of different movement combinations for yourself, about 8 to 12 counts in length, using these means of locomotion. Practice them until you can do them with ease. Name the locomotions aloud as you do them, and have someone watch you to see if you are really doing what you say you are.

Both gesture and locomotion may be either straight or curved in their line of action. The arrival point may be the same, but the itinerary can be different. Take the gesture of reaching the hand forward to shoulder level. The hand starts hanging down by the side. It can travel up the body and forward to shoulder level by means of alternate flexion and extension of the shoulder and elbow joints, describing a path of perpendicular lines. It can also travel in a circular path, as in an arm swing, with a circumduction action at the shoulder joint.

Locomotion, as you have seen, can travel along a circular path in the horizontal or vertical plane. In the horizontal plane, the motion can curve either to the right or the left. In the vertical plane, the curve can be either under or over.

Locomotion in a straight path occurs in any of ten directions. They are: *forward, backward, sideward right, sideward left, forward diagonal right, forward diagonal left, backward diagonal right, backward diagonal left, up,* and *down.* Think of the body as the center from which forces arise and radiate in all directions. No matter which way the body faces, these directions are relative to the body itself (sideward right is always toward the dancer's righthand side).

If all these forces are operating upon the body with equal strength, their effects balance each other out and the body remains in one place. In order to move in any direction, you must think of releasing the force pulling in the opposite direction. For instance, if you wish to go forward, you release the backward energy and give in to the forward one. Of course, these forces, with the exception of gravity (the downward one), are imaginary. But keeping their images in mind lends additional pungency and vitality to the quality of your movement through

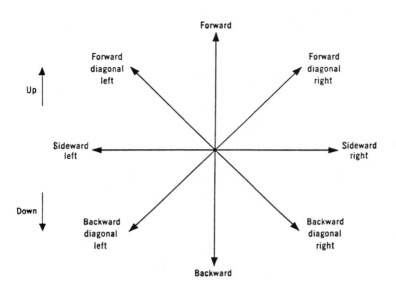

space. Moving into the backward direction is *not* moving away from forward; instead, the forward force is released, and energy is dedicated to the motion backward.

Learning Experiences

Walk forward through space. Be sure that your total attention and total body are forward, with nothing left behind, straying out to the sides, pushing up, or pressing down. Now walk backward in the same way, feeling your whole back press through space. Now go sideward, and feel the pressure of air along the whole side of your body.

Combine four steps forward, four steps sideward right, four steps backward, and four steps sideward left in a square or box pattern. Now use the same arrangement of steps but change your facing in space, so that all your steps follow one straight line across the floor.

To summarize, in order for motion to occur, the weight must be shifted in the direction of the desired motion. To maintain balance, the weight must be directly above the base of support, counteracting the downward pull of gravity. This holds true for almost any locomotion that uses the feet as a base of support.

Learning Experience

Practice walking, running, and other locomotions with different placements of your chest. Try them with your chest over the base of support — then in front of it, then

*behind it. Note what compensations you have to make with other parts of the body
to keep from falling. Notice the different rates of speed at which you can move with
these various chest placements.*

---

7. For dance, the fullest movement potential of the body should be developed.

In modern dance, there are really no right and wrong movements. There are
those movements that are better for general use than others because they are
more efficient, more harmonious to the body's structure, and more pleasing to
watch, but these usages are not absolute, and they can be deliberately distorted
if that is the effect you wish to create.

One of your goals as a dancer is to be able to use your body in any way you
decide, within its capabilities. You may have discovered from past experience
that there are certain movements and controls that require skills you do not yet
have. The greatest facility in movement requires the greatest range of motion
in your joints, the greatest refinement of your movement-producing muscles,
adequate strength in the muscles bearing greatest stress, and a carefully
developed sense of rhythm and balance. Which of these skills can be developed
if you do not already possess them? By hard work and continual attention, all
of these can be developed to a degree limited only by the structure of each
individual body. Adequate body facility includes lengthening of the muscles of
the back, backs of the legs, and insides of the legs; it also includes strengthening
of the muscles of the abdomen, back, thighs, calves, hips, and feet. Careful
strengthening and stretching also helps to keep us in a safe and healthy state,
more likely to avoid injury to joints and muscles. The necessary coordination
and sense of rhythm is the result of practice involving all parts of the body
working together, as well as the soloing of individual parts.

Books and teachers can provide exercises or techniques for developing these
capacities. By shifting your mental focus, you can use these technical tools in
many ways. You should always have a particular point of view about even the
simplest exercise you do, so that you know what it is you want from that exercise
and can focus your concentration on getting it. Even in the simple plié, you may
focus on the totality of movement down and up, outward rotation of the thighs,
release of the lower spine, lengthening of the neck, balance of body parts in their
verticality, the ease of the chest and arms, placement of weight on the soles of
the feet, inner muscular sensations anywhere in the body, to name just a few
areas of concern. The possibilities are limitless; this is why the dancer can keep
finding new mysteries, new delights, and new benefits in the daily warm-up year
after year. It takes a great deal of intelligence and sensitively aware hard work
to attain a responsive and expressive body instrument, but many have felt that
it was worth it. The rewards do not wait until the end, but happen daily in the

delight of a balance held a few seconds longer, an intricate coordination mastered, or the total fulfillment of a gesture.

However, the strengths and flexibilities resulting from these techniques may not be very meaningful to you unless you really need them in actualizing a movement pattern or dance idea. No one is really too impressed by your ability to put your ankle over your ear, and this has little to do with dance. Technique is not an end in itself, but only a means to allow you to do whatever you want to do to the fullest extent. A skilled body is akin to a well-polished car with a well-tuned motor without a driver and with no place to go. When you are the one driving and when you have your own direction, then you will know what is required for the trip and will prepare ahead for it.

4

The Abstract Elements of Dance

CONCEPT: *Sensitive and particular selection and shaping of the abstract elements of dance are what determines it as art.*

Preparing the body for dance is no more art than is a pianist's learning five-finger exercises. This is the craft: the mechanics that allow you to assemble the elements of your art skillfully. It is the elements of the art, rather than its craft, with which you will now be concerned.

Dance, and indeed all movement, happens in a space, uses up time, and requires energy. These are the abstract elements of the art. In the following pages there are experiences that will acquaint you with the several facets of these elements, allow you to experiment with them in your own way, and sharpen your artistic judgment in regard to their use in your dances.

Art starts when you begin to be concerned with other than the body instrument and the work done: when you are careful about and sensitive to the space you use, the time you take, and the energy you exert in making shapes with your body and lines in space. When you are concerned not just with getting to the destination, but more with how you get there, you begin to dance.

The following pages include many experiences in the abstract elements of dance. Try them all. Try some of them more than once, changing the emphasis of the problem from one aspect to another.

1. **The aspects of space must be studied and explored for clear and meaningful movement.**

The space you have to work *in* as a dancer is, simply, all the space that happens to surround you on the stage, in the studio, in the gymnasium, or wherever your work area may be. The space you have to work *with* is a different matter. This space is extremely flexible. In fact, you can make it appear or disappear at will, through your skill in creating illusions. Through different emphases, you can make your audience actually see what they might otherwise regard as empty space. You can create objects in space, within the viewers' imaginations and yours, and destroy them just as readily. You can even make spaces within spaces.

Shape is the three-dimensional space concern of the total body. Shape is one of the strongest visual components of dance. It is present in every moment of every motion, and it is one of the things that the viewer's eye retains longest after the performance is over. Shape is the sculptural design of a body, a group of bodies, or bodies and their prop or costume extensions. The spatial relationships of the bodies or of their component parts create the sculptural shapes.

Shapes are lines and angles, chunks and masses. While you are concerned with the look of these shapes from the outside, you will be concerned also with the kinesthetic feeling of these shapes.

Your body, by virtue of having a number of long, straight bones, is naturally facile at making shapes with straight lines and angles.

Learning Experience

Using the mirror if you wish, design at least ten straight-line shapes for your body. Sense the muscular feel of each shape and check the mirror for the visual impact it might make on an audience. Now design ten more straight shapes without the use of the mirror, sensing only through your body how the shapes must look from the outside.

Straight diagonal line design.

Softer, curved shapes are also possible. You already have a series of natural curves in your spine, and even the angular arms and legs can, by illusion, be formed into curves by using only a slight degree of flexion.

Learning Experience

Repeat the above experience, using curved shapes. To begin with, start the curve in the center of your torso, using your deep central muscles to produce it. Then let the curve find its way out into the periphery.

Explore as many shape variations as possible with your own body. You can make slim or wide shapes, harmonious or dissonant shapes, solid shapes or shapes with holes in them. Try to relate different body parts in unusual ways — a knee to an earlobe, an elbow to a hip bone.

Learning Experience

Make at least 25 of the most diverse shapes with your body. Be aware of the kinesthetic feel of each shape.

Do not preplan your shapes. The most exciting moments often occur when you act first and think about it afterwards. The body has a way of taking over, if you let it, and the spontaneous things that happen are often far more interesting than anything you could plan intellectually. In fact, accidents are the way almost all original things are created because the mind tends to think first of things already experienced.

Learning Experience

Improvise on the idea of shape. Spend your time between shapes not planning the next one, but sensing how it feels to be in the present one. Shorten the time interval between shapes, until you are doing a new shape every second or two. Do not give yourself time to preplan them.

When you dance alone, it is easy for an audience to see your shape, as it is outlined by the space surrounding it. Your intrusion into bare space breaks that space up into smaller pieces, which themselves are shapes. Try standing with your legs in a wide sideward stride. Now you have created a triangular space, bounded by your two legs and the floor. You yourself have a shape, and that space which you have created also has a shape. In art, this is sometimes referred to as *negative space*. Change the shape of that space between your legs and the floor.

As you work with more people, the resulting shapes become increasingly complex. We see the shape of a single tree in a meadow by the shape of the space around it and the negative spaces between the leaves and branches. What makes a tree difficult to see in a forest is the lack of surrounding negative space. As you work with a partner, and finally with a group, be sensitive to the negative spaces created by your positive body shapes.

Learning Experiences

Work in pairs. Partner A makes a shape. Partner B relates to that shape by fitting into one or more of the negative spaces created by A's shape. Partner B holds this shape, while A pulls out of the original shape and fits into the negative spaces created by B. Both will leave some negative spaces free, so that the resulting combined shape can be clearly seen.

Try this experience with three or more dancers. Remember that as more people are added, the total shape will become more complicated, and therefore each individual shape should be kept simple. Keep enough negative spaces in the design so that it makes a coherent whole, rather than a miscellaneous tangle of arms and legs (unless you want a comedy).

Group tangle: total shape of individual shapes.

Stationary shapes are fine, but rarely do you dance standing still. Finding a way to move through space and still retain the character of your shape can be fun. You might be able to locomote on two feet, or you might have to travel on other bases of support.

Learning Experiences

Improvise with shape, moving across the floor. Design a shape before starting, and see how you can travel through space and still hold the shape you have made. Try some shapes on a two-footed base. Try some shapes that rest on other parts of your body besides your feet. How can these shapes travel?

Try the preceding experience with a partner. See what adjustments are caused by your spatial dependence upon one another as you try to locomote in your combined shape.

In order for dance to occur, shapes must change. Movement occurs in going from one to the next. Though no formula can be set down for finding the best way for a shape to begin to move, by and large the motion which seems the most natural is a good one to choose. Another possibility is a motion that begins from the focal point of the shape itself. For instance, consider the shape of the body in its normal standing position, but with the head tilted to one side. The focal point of this shape is obviously the strange placement of the head and the neck.

Complementary and contrasting shapes.

Because they are at odds with the rest of the shape, and with the body as you are accustomed to seeing it, your attention is immediately drawn to that area. It would seem logical, then, that the first movement of that shape might start somewhere in the neck, rather than in an arbitrary place like a foot or hand. One clue to finding the focal point of a shape, though not always accurate, is to find the place of strongest kinesthetic feeling in the body. In the shape just described, the muscular sensation in the neck is quite strong, fairly shouting that this is the place where motion should begin.

Learning Experiences

Start in the shape shown in the first photograph on page 54 and find where to go from there. Listen to your body. Hold the position long enough to know where the focal point of the shape lies, then continue from there. Go from there into the next logical shape, experiencing each progressive change and knowing how other shapes should continue. Try the same procedure with the next two photographs.

Make at least 15 body shapes of your own and devise their first movements. Discover where the movements should start and what those movements should be. Repeat the experience, in dual shapes, with a partner. Try to sense, without verbal communication, where the first motion of your combined shape would begin.

The dancer in motion is like a moving picture. If you stopped the film, or the dancer, at any given moment there would be a frozen shape in the arrested motion. Although dancers may be aware of the more obvious shapes that they are making, they must also be aware of the continuously changing shapes that they make en route — that is, in transition from one shape to another.

Learning Experiences

Design two different shapes. Then devise a way of getting from the first to the second, starting the motion at its most logical place in your body and proceeding as directly as possible to the second shape.

Design a series of ten shapes. Create movement transitions to link these shapes.

Shape, then, is one aspect of space that is always present in dance — as you can see in the stop-action of a film. Dancers may emphasize or de-emphasize shape, depending on their purpose, but they should be aware of its presence in all motion.

Shapes: 3-D twist.   *2-D flat.*

3-D hovering.

The body in motion can carve a shaped volume of space out of the surrounding area. *Volume* is an aspect of space that is somewhat related to shape, but it concerns itself primarily with negative or surrounding space, rather than with the positive space of the dancer's body. Because volume is created out of negative space, it is up to the dancer to establish the dimensions of that volume for the audience and to make them see it as if it actually existed.

Volume can be said to be a piece of space encompassed by boundaries. A volume can exist anywhere in the space through which a dancer moves. The dancer defines the boundaries, either partially or wholly, by using the body, and therefore defines the volume.

As an example, consider the shape of your arms as they form a circle in front of your chest, parallel to the floor. They create the partial boundaries of a volume of space. The volume might be spherical, as if you were holding a beachball, or it might be cylindrical, as if you were enclosing a tall column. You could further define the exact shape of that volume through motion. Now bring your arms out to shoulder level. There are several possibilities here. You might deal with the volume of space between your arms and the floor. You could compress or expand that volume. You could lift or lower the volume of space above your arms, or even carry it through space with you. Through your imaginative use of movement, you can create, change, or even destroy any volume you wish in the space around you.

Learning Experience

Improvise with six different arm placements. Consider them the partial boundaries of a volume of space. See how many different volumes you can create with each position. Do the same with the volume created by six different leg arrangements.

Volumes of space can be created between any parts of your body. Do not be confined to arms and legs. You can create volumes between your legs and chest, between your arm and your side, or between your head and the floor. You need not describe the total boundary of the volume. Often a partial indication will be enough to establish its size.

Learning Experiences

Improvise with volume as your main idea. Create volumes in space. Change the size of these volumes.

With a partner, experiment with creating volumes between the two of you. Change the size, shape, and location of the volumes. Expand them; compress them.

Sometimes you may wish to establish a volume in space, go away from it, and then return to it. If your definition of the volume is sufficiently strong, you can make the audience see that volume as still existing where you put it, even if you leave it for a while.

Learning Experiences

Work with an actual object — a box, a table, a bench, or other simple prop. Define its volume. You may want to trace its outline with your hands, for example, or its height by sitting on it. Be very clear in your definition. Now remove the actual object and establish the same volume in space. Be just as clear in defining its boundaries.

Work in a group. Have several objects scattered in the working space. They should be objects which can be moved on, under, or through. Establish the shape of each object in space. Now remove the actual objects and restate their volumes in space. Move among them as if they still occupied their former spaces — in other words, be careful not to walk through a table.

Again, work in a group. Establish a volume in space, perhaps a simple geometric figure. Through movement, indicate its boundaries. You may work outside or inside the volume. Now move it from place to place. Change its position in space, but do not destroy the form.

The space around you, as you know, is not really empty. It is full of moleculres, as is everything made of matter. The higher the concentration of molecules, the greater the *density* of the matter. The air in the space around you is not very dense; you find it relatively easy to move through it. Yet, through your performing skill, you can create the illusion of density of space. Use your past experiences and your imagination to help you. Almost all people have had the experience of trying to walk through water. What were some of the physical changes in your movement which were caused by the density of the water? How might you move if there were no resistance at all to your motion?

Learning Experience

Improvise with at least three different densities of space. Establish each density in a given section of your working space. As you move from "thick" to "medium" to "thin," let your motion reflect the changing density of the surrounding space.

The dimension of a movement must be carefully defined for clarity of meaning. *Dimension* in dance is the definition of the space in which you work — its height, its width, and its depth.

Images of flatness, 2 dimensional space.

While your work with shapes requires that you design in three dimensions, it is also possible to think about motion specifically in these different dimensions of space. The depth dimension includes the directions of forward and backward; the width dimension includes the sideward directions, while the height dimension deals with the directions of up and down. It's interesting to think about the plié, for instance, in terms of dimension. It is basically concerned with height, the verticality of up and down. But practiced in second position, with feet apart and arms wide, it also involves the width dimension; when done in fourth position, one foot ahead of the other and opposite arm forward, you are also aware of the depth dimension. You're concerned with forward and back. Your specific use of space can produce various effects. Limiting movement to a sideward dimension might be one way to qualify the space around you. By setting up limits such as this when dealing with a movement problem, you will often find the most exciting solutions.

Learning Experiences

Limit yourself to the exploration of a two-dimensional space — forward and backward, side to side, diagonally, or up and down. Keep your body thin and narrow, and the motion as nearly as possible in a two-dimensional plane. Improvise.

Working with a partner, improvise in the same two-dimensional plane. (The addition of another person can amplify dimensional experiences.)

Again, work with a partner, each in a two-dimensional space, but in contrasting dimensions — depth against width or diagonal against vertical.

One aspect of the height dimension is *level*. In modern dance you can work in any level of the space that you can reach, from prone on the floor to the greatest height you can jump. With the aid of prop extensions, you might reach even higher. For the most part, though, when you move on your feet, you move in one of three levels — low, middle, and high. Middle level is your normal walking level. Low level occurs when you move in plié; high level when you use your feet in relevé. Of course, nothing in your improvisations limits you to moving only on your feet.

Learning Experience

Singly, in partners, or in a group, explore the space parallel to the floor at different levels. Sense the movement at each plane, the parallel relationship to the floor and the relative distances from the floor to the various levels.

Another aspect of dimension is *distance*. When you decide to move into a forward direction, you must immediately make another decision — how far? An inch? A foot? As far away as you can reach? Farther than you can reach? There is enormous room for variation in the size of a movement, from a purely physical standpoint. You can make a forward gesture of the hand that involves the most minute movement of the wrist, or you can make one for which the whole body must wind up to project that hand forward in space. You can cover a gigantic amount of space with a leap or a sweep of your arm, or do crochet-like gestures with fingers while moving along with the tiniest of steps. Such contrasts keep us interested and can provide a wonderful, comic effect.

Learning Experience

Explore the possibilities of various sizes of movements. Find large movements for small parts of your body and small movements for large parts. Using one body part, begin with small motion, progress to larger motion and back down to small — both gradually and suddenly. Make large movements in one body part and small movements in another at the same time. Move with or against another person in large and small relationships.

Contrast in size of movement.

Beyond the physical limits of the body, you have additional means to achieve enormous distance. By projecting the psyche into space at the same time, you can create the illusion of limitless distance. The totality of the coordination between the psyche and the body is primarily responsible for the phenomenon of *projection*. Spatial projection is but one facet of total performing projection.

Learning Experience

Make a short dance phrase. Treat the space around you in three different ways as you perform the phrase. Emphasize the space: (1) one foot away from you; (2) as far as you can reach; (3) to infinity.

The floor pattern of a dance influences its aesthetic effect. As you move through space during a dance, you trace a pattern through that space; this is sometimes called the *floor pattern*. If you had wet paint on your feet, this floor pattern would be obvious at a single glance. The audience sees this floor pattern not at one glance, but gradually — in time — as you make it. Floor patterns can be more or less important, depending on the dance. You should be aware of their existence, so that you may use them to advantage and avoid their pitfalls. Keep your floor patterns interesting. Unless it is your particular aim to impress your audience with monotony, do not choreograph a whole dance in circles.

Learning Experience

Devise for yourself, by moving or drawing, a floor pattern of walks that goes in most of the eight horizontal directions (see page 47). Include some curved paths, if you wish, either horizontal or vertical ones. Then, using the same floor pattern, choreograph more interesting locomotor movements to substitute for the walks. Finally, choreograph the rest of your body's movements to complement the locomotor movements you have devised. Perform the three separate facets of this experience. Try to retain the clarity of of your original floor pattern, even though the movement on top of it has become more complex.

The floor pattern can determine the motional line of a body. A strong run in a straight diagonal path requires almost a straight forward diagonal lean of the body. On the other hand, the floor pattern can be an outgrowth of the shape or motional line of the body. If a movement begins in the curving of the torso and zig-zagging of the arms, a later development of this pattern may carry out the use of the original curve and zig-zag in its floor pattern.

Learning Experiences

Choose a shape, perhaps a good one from your recent experiences in shape. Retain it long enough to realize the linear implications within it. Then develop a locomotor pattern from this shape, using the lines of that shape as a pattern for your floor design.

A shape to design from.

Finally, having experienced space in all these various ways, choreograph a short study in which space is your main focus. Project this element to your viewers, above and beyond all others. Make them aware of space, rather than of motion, energy, time, or you.

2. Time is an organizing factor in movement and in choreography.

Dance, as well as every other activity in this world, occurs in *time*. Again, the time you have to work *in* is all the time you have to give to your work. The time you have to work *with* is immediate or infinite, but it will be a piece of time carved out for your particular purpose. A dance has a beginning, and 30 seconds later, or 3 minutes later, or an hour later, it has an end. What goes on in the dance within that time span may be slow or fast. It will be sensed as slow or fast by the motion of the body within that one piece of time. If the piece lasts for 3 minutes and you fill it with ten movements, slowness will probably be sensed. If you fill it with 300 movements, fastness will be the result. Two aspects of time with which you will be concerned next are *duration* and *speed*.

The quality of motion is affected very definitely by its duration. As you become more and more sensitive to your own motion, you become aware of how long each motion lasts. It may be a fraction of a second, or it may be a full minute or even longer. Swing your arms in a full circle in 1 second. Make the same motion again, but take 1 minute to complete it. Walk around the room, taking two steps every second. Then try taking five seconds for each step, and then ten seconds for each step.

No doubt the muscular feel of the motions of short duration were much different from the feel of those which took a long time. You may have recognized totally different qualities, even though the motions themselves were essentially the same, except for their time values.

Learning Experience

Select four or five different actions that are simple to perform, such as rolling, walking, standing up, sitting down, scratching, and stopping. Perform any of these actions at any time you wish, and for as long as you wish. Sense the duration of each action and experiment with extremes of long and short duration. Be just as sensitive to the duration of the stops as you are to the actions.

To be able to sense how long a movement should continue is a valuable skill for a dancer. To sense how long a coffee break, a visit, or a friendship should go on is a valuable skill for anyone. Sensitizing yourself to duration in movement should make you more aware of the whole pace of your life.

In many dances, metered music tells you exactly how long a movement should be — half a beat, two beats, or six beats. But it is likely that there will be times when there is no metrical beat to help you. Some modern choreographers create with a stop watch instead of a musical score. They determine that certain movements or phrses should last a given amount of time. Through repeated rehearsals, the dancers learn to judge these lengths of time with amazing accuracy. Music, or sound, is then composed in equivalent time units for the dance.

Learning Experiences

Work with a partner. Set an arbitrary duration, such as 20 seconds. Keep moving for what you believe to be 20 seconds, then stop. Your partner, armed with a stop watch or a watch with a second hand, will let you know how close you came to hitting the mark. Practice with a number of different durations.

Perform a movement combination that moves across the floor. Practice doing it with one or two other people, using no beat or accompaniment of any kind. Learn to sense the common duration of each movement, so that ultimately you are all moving simultaneously.

A sense of duration is particularly helpful to you in improvisation. Movement themes that are started in an improvisation need a certain amount of time to establish themselves. If this time is allowed to drag on too long, boredom sets in. If it is not long enough, a feeling of frustration and unfulfillment results. Try to be aware of this in your next improvisation. Try to find the "right" time to start a fresh action.

Speed determines its own use of energy and the feeling of movement. *Speed,* of course, is the fastness or slowness of a motion. The range between faster-than-fast and slower-than-slow can be very great. Your ability to perform these extremes of speed may be greater than you think.

Learning Experience

Perform several single movements as fast as you possibly can — so fast that the eye can barefly follow them. Notice the change in expenditure of energy and the feel of the movement. Now try a movement as slowly as you can make it. See if you can move so slowly as to be almost imperceptible, like the minute hand of the clock.

Of course, you will not want to move slower-than-slow or faster-than-fast in every dance, but these tempos should be available to you when you want them. You will usually use a variety of speeds, some of them extreme. Nothing kills interest quicker than moderation. A good brisk accent in a series of slow movements, or a sudden sustained movement in the midst of a driving tempo can do wonders to enliven the audience, the dancer, or the vitality of the movement itself.

Learning Experience

Improvise freely by yourself, simply being aware of the speed of your motion. Try abrupt changes from slow to fast. Try gradual acceleration. Try coming out of a very fast movement immediately into a very slow one.

Speed and duration are, of course, interrelated. A fast movement has a short duration. A single movement of long duration will understandably be slow.

A fast motion above a still one.

Sometimes movements are repetitious, though, and a series of fast movements can last for a long time.

Single actions join other single actions into longer units known as *phrases.* A phrase may be of any duration and any speed, or several speeds. A phrase may consist of any number of separate motions, but its distinguishing feature is that it has a sense of semicompletion about it. Longer and longer time units occur as a dance progresses — phrases join to become a *section;* sections may join to become separate *acts* of an evening-length ballet; and finally, all the time units join to make a whole dance. A dance may be no more than a minute or no less than a full evening in length. Its duration will be determined by its content. When it feels completed, it is done; it lasts as long as it *should* last.

When we discuss duration, it is useful to borrow some terms from music, particularly terms used to describe rhythm. *Meter* describes the number of *beats* in a *measure* of music. For example, in 4/4 time, there are 4 *beats* to a measure; every fourth beat may receive a heavier *accent* or emphasis, to mark the beginning of a measure. This meter will remain unchanged throughout a phrase or an entire work of music. In order to determine the meter of a piece of music, you must identify each beat and *count* the number of beats per measure.

Learning Experience

Try identifying the meter of some common melodies. For example, listen to "The Blue Danube Waltz." Can you pick out the distinctive ONE-two-three ONE-two-three meter of 3/4 waltz time? Now listen to "Bad" by Michael Jackson. Can you identify its meter?

Using this kind of *metered time* in dance, it is easy to tell the duration of a movement by counting the number of beats it occupies. Once the rate of speed of the beat is established, one has only to count off as many beats as are needed to know how long each particular movement lasts. Metered time is a convenient way to mark off time, particularly for a group of dancers; everyone is moving to the same time standard, so keeping together is no problem.

You can alter time as you alter space, by a particular use of movement. You can divide it into equal units and repeated rhythms, or into unequal units and different rhythms. It can appear to flow on, to stop altogether, or to be broken up into chunks. A particular use of time will alter your movement. Tensions are created by gradually accelerating the speed of motion or by gradually shortening the units of division.

Every movement will have its own characteristic rhythmic structure. If you are tuned in to it, you can almost count out in consistent organization the rhythm of brushing your teeth or starting your car. Each activity has its own rhythm; even each feeling has its own rhythm because of the way it affects the heart and breathing apparatus.

Learning Experiences

Take an everyday activity and repeat it until you can do it without thinking about it, doing it consistently the same way every time. Now have someone clap a pattern of accents for you. Using this rhythmic pattern, find a new movement combination for it.

Build a rhythmic pattern, or use this one:

and find a movement pattern to fit it. Repeat the movement pattern enough times to sense the kinesthetic feeling that accompanies the rhythm.

Even though you will find that each motion falls into its own natural rhythmic pattern, it does not mean that you must be true to that pattern all the time. In dance, it is your privilege to alter movement characteristics. Doing familiar movements in erratic time patterns may result in a fascinating dance.

When you work with metered time, you will base your organization on an underlying *pulse* — a steady, even beat which is continuous. These beats can be separated into different group lengths by capitalizing the first beat in each group with an accent and by putting periods at the end of each phrase. Just as the words on this page are punctuated with commas, periods, and semicolons, movement may be punctuated with changes of direction, sudden jumps, or force accents. Phrases may begin with a bang and end logically with a period, or they may begin slowly and end suddenly in an exclamation point!

Learning Experience

Using a walk or run, move in 3/4 time, accenting the first of each three beats by stamping, clapping, or taking lower, longer. or higher steps. Change direction on the first beat; jump on it. Do the same with 5/4 time. Notice the difference in feeling. Try the same thing with 4/4 time, and compare the feeling of this with the others. Now put together combinations of fives, fours, and threes in ascending or descending order, or mixed.

Sometimes metered time is simply undesirable for a dance or an improvisation. Time can then be loosely structured or timed in seconds. In this case, the dancer's intuition is relied upon to judge how fast and how long to move. When working with a group, it takes practice and sensitivity for all to establish a common time denominator without relying on a metrical beat. Such loosely structured time often allows for greater spontaneity between the dancer and the movement than does more organized, metered time.

Learning Experiences

Improvise freely to a metrical drum beat or to a piece of music. Move with the regularity of the beat. Now try to move against it. Alternate phrases that are "in time" with phrases that are "out of time".

Improvise with no beat at all on the subject of "move and stop." Be particularly sensitive to the speed with which you move, to the duration of your movement, to the silence you hear, and to the length of the times when you hold still.

Work with a partner or in threes, having conversations in rhythms. Let one person start and the next react. Keep the rhythmic responses going as you would a verbal conversation. Clap, stamp, or move your conversations. Make voice sounds.

Finally, draw upon the time experiences you have just had and choreograph a short study in which you present "time." Make your viewers see time over and above all other aspects of motion.

---

3. **The amount of energy and method of its expenditure in dance may be determined by the time-space factors or by a particular motivation.**

Energy is closely related to time and space. Slow movement in a small space takes little energy. Moving through a large space in a small amount of time takes lots of energy.

All motion requires energy. Even lying still, just breathing, takes some small effort to keep the diaphragm moving up and down. Energy is merely one of the factors that gives a movement its particular quality.

Two types of energy are of concern to you in your study of dance. One is the obvious, *physical energy* needed to move muscle and bone. The other is *psychic energy*. There is nothing mystical about this psychic energy. It is simply that which lends spirit and vitality to a dancer's motion through means other than physical.

The *physical energy* to move one's body is supplied by the contraction of the muscles. The greater the muscular job, the more energy that is required. To lift the entire weight of the body off the floor in a jump takes a great burst of energy. To raise one arm slowly takes very little. Each motion has its own minimum requirement of energy to accomplish that motion. Any more energy than that minimum makes the performance of the motion inefficient. This inefficiency can occur under two circumstances. One is that the dancer may have planned it that way to produce a particular quality of motion. The other is that the proper amount of energy for performing a particular movement has been overestimated, resulting in excess tension. This should be avoided, as tension will not only make the motion difficult to perform, but will also call attention to itself. The audience will then see the dancer's problems with the movement, rather than the quality of the motion being performed. The only valid reason for executing a movement with more tension than necessary is to alter the quality of the movement.

Learning Experiences

Extend one arm in front of you. Gradually increase the tension in that arm, without moving it, until it is as tense as you can make it. Notice the difference in the appearance of the arm itself. Release the tension quickly. Note the change.

Raise one arm from its normal position sideward to shoulder level. As you do, gradually increase the tension from none at all to very strong. Repeat the same action, starting with a maximum of tension, or energy, in the arm, and as the arm is raised, decreasing it to just enough energy to raise the arm. Perform the entire motion with a minimum of energy, then with a maximum of energy. Watch to see what quality changes occur as a result of the differences in energy.

Explore the sensation of tension. Allow it to build and then release in different parts of the body, and in the total body. In a state of great tension, try a movement pattern you have already done. Notice the change in feeling and its effects on the shape of your body and your breathing.

Finding the proper amount of energy to perform an action efficiently is a skill that has to do with the mechanics of dance. In the art of dance, you will employ your artistic judgment and make choices about how you are going to use energy, not just to perform a motion, but to produce a special quality of motion that you wish to project.

No one can tell you that a certain amount of energy or a certain way of expending it will give you the quality of motion you desire. You have to experiment to find this out for yourself, and others can only suggest what possibilities there may be.

You have a choice of the quantity of energy to use — a lot, a little, or something in between. Of course, you know that the gradations between a lot and a little are many. Then you must choose the way you will spend this energy. Should you attack the movement explosively and let the energy gradually dissipate itself? Should you start gently and gradually build to great strength? Or should the amount of energy you use be the same throughout the movement or the phrase?

Learning Experiences

Improvise on any three of the energy possibilities mentioned in the preceding paragraph. Stay with each one long enough to explore in some depth its potentials for movement. Then intersperse the qualities as you improvise further. Be constantly sensitive to energy.

Compose a short study in which you project energy over all the other elements discussed.

Your manner of releasing the energy you have collected for the movement is also a matter of your aesthetic choice. You may yield to gravity once in a while, in a swing, using only a little energy to pick up the upward tail of the swing. You might sustain a movement, so that no part of it is more or less forceful than another. You can let it out like sand pouring out of a sock, leaving you hollow and empty, or keep it within like a huge secret, giving out only an occasional glimpse of its potential. You might bounce, rebound, vibrate, collapse, shake, or hurl yourself into space. The possibilities are limitless.

Weight also affects the quality or texture of movement. To give in to your weight is to project heaviness in part or in all of you. To make light of your weight is a whole different image and feeling of the motion.

Learning Experience

Give weight to the head, the shoulder, then the hip, in sequence. Lift and lower each leg, each arm, experiencing each as heavy. Now breathe into these limbs and lift them as though they were weightless, or helium-filled, as though they might float away from you.

Projecting the idea of weight in upper body.

Magic can be made by playing with these energies and weights, by projecting different realities, by creating illusions. The dancer is a maker of magic and can make watchers see and believe most anything. Part of this ability has to do with *psychic energy.*

Psychic energy is that intangible commodity which, it is said, gives life to your dancing. Like life, it is almost impossible to define. It might be defined as a spirit of vitality within you, a strongly felt motivation to do and to move, an enthusiasm of the will, a projection of your mental self beyond your physical self. It is a state of being immediately present — of being mentally with your physical self in time, and not an instant behind or ahead of it. However it is defined, its presence or absence is immediately discernible in your ability to project movement. This magic of projection presents itself as a light in your eye, an extra millimeter of lift in your sternum, a feeling of totality and fulfillment of a motion, an illusion made credible.

The psyche is even more mobile than your physical self. You can withdraw it inside you, or project it out into infinity. It can ride on the surface of your skin, or shoot out through the top of your head. Take the trouble to find yours. No one can tell you how, but you might begin by looking inside yourself — by practicing internal awareness and sensitivity to the world around you, and to that "electricity" which connects you to all living things.

The elements of time, space, and energy cannot be separated except for discussion. You do not make a single movement without using each one, and all simultaneously. The awareness of all these elements and their effect on each other make you aware of the possibilities of your art. You move with quality — the result of the sensitive use of time, space, and energy in totally realized motion.

Learning Experience

Putting it all together: Having experienced at least some of the many possibilities of movement, design a combination of gestures and locomotion which goes somewhere in space, makes its own statement in time, and uses energy in a particular way. This combination should be satisfying to do, have contrast and order, and a sense of wholeness about it. Repeat this several times, reworking it until it is very comfortable and satisfying to do. We will call this a phrase, *a movement sentence, the first small unit of choreography.*

5

Improvisation

CONCEPT: Improvisation is an indispensable and exciting part of the dance experience.

Improvisation — creating on the spur of the moment — is an essential part of every creative art. The artist makes preliminary sketches before painting. The musician experiments with combinations of sounds. For the dancer, movement improvisation is a prelude to choreography. It is also a tool for developing an individual's performing sensitivity and a means of discovering the body's natural movement style, and it has potentiality as an art in its own right.

1. Improvisation can be of two kinds — *structured* or *completely free*.

In free improvisation, no subject matter is decided upon beforehand, no boundaries set, and no limits imposed. You simply turn yourself on and begin to move, letting the improvisation progress continuously in any direction that may suggest itself as you go along. Your spontaneous response to previous material or your own present state of being and awareness directs the course of the improvisation. With free improvisation, you are likely to touch upon a broad spectrum of movement subjects, but there is a danger inherent in this way of working. With an unlimited subject, it is tempting to skim over the surface, doing the most obvious movements or the ones that come most naturally to your particular movement style. This is especially likely to happen at the beginning of the improvisation. You must persist for long enough to get out of this stylistic groove. Your body will ultimately become bored with the same old things; it is only then that fresh, new things will begin to happen.

For the beginner a limited improvisational situation is easier to handle. This kind of improvisation is more highly structured. Until you are well practiced in the skills of improvisation, it will be wisest for you to work within limitations. These will be set ahead of time with reference to the subject matter of the improvisation. During improvisation, you respond not only to previous movement material, but continually in reference to the original problem. Keeping your improvisation related to the original problem will allow you to experience one thing in great depth, while in free improvisation, you may only skim the surface of a lot of things in serial order. It is in experiencing something in depth that you go beyond the most obvious, ordinary, comfortable movements and extend the range of your possibilities. You may use the problems suggested in this book or by your instructor, or you may originate your own. Devising your own is probably most desirable because ultimately this is the way the mature artist works.

An improvisation almost has a life of its own. If you are open and allow the situation to take over, rather than try to force it in a direction you want to go, you will be much more likely to have a new experience. After all, you grow only through new experiences and your reactions to these experiences. An improvisation is a situation that allows you to have a new experience, and the limits of the problem are the framework in which the experience can occur.

2. Improvisation serves many personal and dance needs.

Improvisation is a major part of your dance training and a valuable experience for anyone. Its purposes are many. For some of you, it may be the first creative experience you have had since childhood. Ask yourself how long it has been since you have relied completely on your imagination. You used to spend hours playing house, scribbling on blank pieces of paper, or humming little tunes that you made up as you went along. As you grew older, you played games with prescribed rules, followed coloring book lines that someone else had drawn, or sang songs that you learned in school. As an adult, your participation in art probably consists of reading, going to plays, concerts, and galleries, or perhaps playing an instrument — but playing music written by someone else. What has happened to your own imagination along the way? Where is the spontaneity with which you used to get up a game of cops and robbers?

In improvisation, you are once again dependent on your own resources to tell you what to do. You have a chance to dust off that imagination and see if it still works. After a little practice, you will probably be surprised at how well it works. This opportunity to take that aspect of your mind out of mothballs may be one of the most valuable experiences you ever have. Let us see how improvisation serves you specifically in dance.

Knowledge of yourself is one of the more important functions of improvisation. You possess a unique body, so you cannot successfully take someone else's movement style and impose it on your own body. Through improvisation you experiment with your own instrument, exploring the limits of its capacity and discovering its natural style. Equally important, you explore the depths of your own imagination.

Choreography seldom takes place without being preceded by a great deal of improvisation, searching for movement materials. This is the "trial and error" method of the artist, and a good 90% of the improvised material is ultimately thrown out. The small percentage that is kept represents the choreographer's selection of the best material. Improvisation may give you ideas for new dances or indicate ways of progressing within a dance. A successful dance is rarely composed cerebrally, without improvisation. The body has a way of finding fresh, pertinent things of which the intellect would never have thought. The more you improvise before choreographing, the greater your chance of originality.

Improvisation is an agent of movement sensitivity. One of the important results of improvisation is the development of your sensitivity — sensitivity to time, to space, to energy, to yourself, to other people, and to motion. This sensitivity is possible only when you concentrate fully on the present moment of the improvisation — a state of being totally "in" it. Being "in" it is not a state of being lost in the improvisation beyond all awareness of outside considerations, but a state in which all these things are less important than the improvisation. When you are "in" it, you are no longer concerned with how you look, what is coming next, whether you will lose your balance, or whether your toe is pointed or not. You are totally dedicated to the improvisation and to your sensing of it. When you are not "in" it, you appear to be mentally on the outskirts of the improvisation. It is as if your mind were once removed from the proceedings, even though your body may be there. You are not "in" until your mind and body function as one at the same instant.

The "in" condition is the one that makes you shine in performance, so you want to be sure to recognize it, as well as its absence. How do you get "in"? First of all, forget yourself. Focus on other people. Focus on the movement, on the quality of the movement, on the timing. Second, allow yourself to be swept along by the improvisation. Forget trying to do something clever and original. Third, tune in to the sensation of the dominant quality of the improvisational movement.

By forcing you to "think" on your feet, often before other people, improvisation develops your performance awareness. You are required to become aware not only of what you are experiencing at the moment, but also of the need to communicate that experience to an audience by your performance. Awareness of total environment includes other dancers, so a valuable feeling of rapport with them is gained through group improvisation.

Improvisation can attain art status. Finally, improvisation may be an artistic end in itself. Its performance before an audience may be fully as satisfying as a finished piece of choreography. In the beginning, your improvisations will contain a lot of deadwood. They will be full of movement clichés, dynamically dull, trite, and obvious. They will also contain tremendously exciting moments when you discover a movement for the first time, when some motion or relationship creates a moment of aesthetic delight, or when an audience sees a movement for the first time. As you become more skilled at improvisation, the percentage of deadwood decreases and the moments of delight increase. Your developing intuition tells you the right thing to do at the right time. At this point, your improvisation is a spontaneous work of art. It has a real sense of wholeness; it begins, continues in a certain direction, and reaches its own logical conclusion. Within each part, there is a sensitive use of motional elements. There is apparent form and a sensed meaning. When it satisfies all these qualifications, it can be said to be art.

3. Improvisation occurs simply by being allowed to happen.

No one can tell you *how* to improvise. No two improvisations are ever alike, so there is no pat formula that you can follow. There are certain areas that you should leave open to the experience, though — your senses, your intuition, and your memory.

Improvisation requires a degree of subjugation of your own will to the development of the improvisation in the way that is right for it. Your intuition is the only way you have of knowing that rightness. Thinking ahead intellectually is disastrous in improvisation, as it immediately destroys the spontaneity of the action and shows up visibly in the body as something "out" of key.

Although you give your conscious control over to the improvisation, you must not lose conscious awareness of your own response. This is perhaps the most important part of improvisation — your sensing of the experience. Be aware of your feeling for the whole experience, and encourage this by allowing yourself to become a part of it. Begin at the beginning, let the improvisation develop, and end it when you feel as though nothing more should happen. Later, the memory of that sensed experience can be applied to other situations. Develop the skill of recall, as it is important when improvising prior to composition. You may improvise the most stunning movements in the world, but if you cannot recall them they are lost forever.

4. Group improvisation is personally and choreographically enriching.

You will need to improvise alone to discover your own body and your own imagination without the distraction of other dancers. You will also perform improvisation in a group. In this, your major task is to relate to the group as you apply yourselves together to the subject. You relate by being extraordinarily aware of the other dancers and the total environment at all times. You are alert for dynamic changes, for motional changes, for quality changes, and for changes in any and all of the abstract elements of dance. You relate to these changes either by going along with them in a similar vein or by moving in contrast to them. There is never any one right way to respond, but there are some ways that are better than others, so you should learn to recognize them. Seize opportunities to make relationships, but do not force them.

Although you often give over your will to the group, you need not always be a follower. When you sense that a motion or a relationship has gone on too long or is becoming a bore, you may change it and start something else. Others will probably follow your lead if your intuition is right. If you find yourself alone in left field, you have probably misjudged. Lose yourself in the improvisation once more, and better luck next time.

As you improvise for each other in class, you can learn a great deal from watching. Look for those things that are particularly exciting, interesting, and meaningful. Look for what pulls the improvisation together, and look for weak or dull parts. Be aware of contrasts. Were they effective? Too soon? Too much? Did one thing go on too long without variation? Did you see relationships between parts of the whole?

5. Motivations for improvisation are as extensive as life.

The subject matter for improvisation is limitless, ranging from the essence of an owl to the closeness of a group in space, from the essence of adolescence to the mutual support of two dancers. In previous experiences, you have improvised with your body instrument and with the abstract elements of dance. Besides these two important areas, there is another source of dance material. This is the *environment* in which dance exists, and this can serve as the motivation for choreography as well as the final housing for performance.

In the natural experience of the human being, there are continual motor reactions, responses, and adjustments to environment — to lights, sounds, objects, and colors — as well as to other human beings in the environment. These responses are just as meaningful as those made to space, time, and energy elements. Therefore, it is natural for choreographies to grow out of movement relating to any aspect of environment. You might build a dance on the way you could move in a particular costume, in a particular light, or in a special set. Each of these elements will impose certain limitations because of its size, shape, color, intensity, or weight, and will call for a kind of movement that is new and fascinating in itself. For instance, you might start a dance by carrying a long pole and develop a piece out of the relationship of your body to the pole. You might find out how you could move with respect to its function, shape, size, and particular mobility. Here the "idea" of the dance becomes one of your relationship to your physical environment, discovered by your personal moving involvement with it.

Improvisations with these aspects make you at least five times more aware of the world around you. The following improvisations are designed to acquaint you with this environment outside yourself. They will, hopefully, suggest other ideas to you for your own improvisations or dances.

Learning Experiences
With Sets

Discover the shape, size, weight, color, and form of a chair. Shape your body to conform to its design while sitting on the chair. Assume the shape of the chair in other places in space, without using the chair. Find many sitting positions on the chair. Choose four of these and move from one to another, varying fast and slow actions and transitions.

Discover new ways to move around, under, over, and through the chair. How can the chair move? What are its other possible relationships to the floor? How can you move through space with the chair?

Moving in relation to sets.

Build an arrangement, or even a structure, of several chairs. Working with a group, fit yourselves into this arrangement and find new possibilities in the relationships between people and chairs.

Build a structural arrangement of boxes, platforms, ladders, chairs, drapes, or similar objects. Explore movement in and among these objects. Discover the movement potential of the objects. Add other people, and keep them in mind as another element in the total relationship.

Build another architecture of functional objects. People it with dancers who are free not only to move within the structure, but to change its arrangement as they see fit. Relate to the changing environment and to the other dancers.

With Costumes

Move across a space, pulling behind you 15 feet of rayon jersey material. Feel its weight, length, and texture. Let your motion be consonant with the qualities of the cloth. Wear the cloth, roll in it, and let it move as a result of your motion. Treat it as an extension of you, and not as a separate object.

Work in different kinds of costumes: skirts, pillow cases, beach towels, shoes, hats, and other items. Discover the new entity made by you and the costume. Improvise with the costume as a part of you.

With Props

Improvise with a large garment bag. Discover what movement is possible within it. Be aware of the sounds created as you move. Try to visualize what is happening from the outside.

Moving with sensitivity to costume and design.

Moving in relation to props.

Move with a number of functional objects: suitcases, shovels, ladders, toothpicks, and other items. Forget the specific functions of these objects and use them abstractly, responding to their size, shape, weight, or texture.

Improvise with an abstract prop that has no recognizable function.

With Sound

Start a movement sequence with a lift and drop of an arm or leg, followed by a sharp twist. Repeat it, in new directions and with new parts of your body. As you move, be aware of the sounds that accompany the motion because of the way you are forced to breathe or the squeak of your feet on the floor. Exaggerate these sounds and extend them to fill the duration of your movement sequence.

Explore sounds your body can make: snaps, claps, brushes, clicks, or stamps. There is movement necessary to create these sounds. Explore vocal sounds, and move in agreement with them. Finally, discover what sounds are available from objects in the room, and the motion necessary to make them. Improvise in a group, relating to each other in sound and motion.

Use words or nonsense syllables for their sound value, and not for any literal meaning they may have. Improvise in a group, using verbalization as accompaniment.

Improvise, using recorded electronic music (such as Varèse's Poème
Electronique*) as motivation. Allow the individual sounds to motivate movement.
Then move to the more generally sensed essence of the piece. Maintain the movements and their quality, and try them again to a completely different kind of
musical background. Be aware of the resultant feeling.*

With People

*You may have found that your reaction to other people is one of the most fascinating
factors in improvisation and that interrelationships between people can produce the
most meaningful materials for choreography. Other people are perhaps the most
important influence on us in our daily life, so their significance for dance is only
natural. It is important to develop added sensitivity to others in movement
situations.*

Moving with another.

Watch individual people as they sit, stand, and walk, and attempt to imitate them exactly in order to increase your awareness of the characteristic movement styles of others in your group.

Work with a partner. Face each other as you would your reflection in a mirror. Establish a line between you to represent that mirror. Improvise slowly, being sensitive to the shapes being made, to your relative distances from the mirror, and to the fidelity with which you reflect each other's image. Let the initiation of movement pass from partner to partner, with no verbal communication. Try to move simultaneously.

Working with a partner, improvise on the premise that you must maintain physical contact at some point throughout the improvisation. The contact point may change, but try to explore the possibilities of each one thoroughly before changing. Begin with your eyes closed, and sense each other without the aid of your vision. When you are sufficiently tuned in to one another, open your eyes and continue.

In groups of threes, begin in a relationship with contact. Hold your position until something has to move. Let the improvisation proceed from that first impulse into whatever is possible and special for groups of three. Allow it to stop when it is finished.

Standing in a circle, make contact somehow with those on each side and hold the position of contact. As weights and pulls become noticeable, allow yourself to go in the direction indicated, but gently and carefully, so as not to destroy the circle. Let the improvisation unfold until it comes to a natural end.

Standing in a closely packed group so that all are somehow touching while facing forward, tune in to the group pulse. Be aware of the lift and fall of breathing bodies. Be aware of the natural postural sway and do not restrain it. When you feel pressures on your body, allow subtle changes in your own position to occur, and then be open to whatever may happen next. Try to be so sensitively attuned that the group moves as one body with one mind.

Design a group arrangement in which people are related in space because of the way they are facing; use only the four walls for directions. Improvise by merely walking or changing level. The body stays upright, movement can go only up and down or toward the walls, direction can change and one may travel forward, backward, or sideways. Tempos also may vary. Be aware of the close interrelationship experienced here, and of the feeling of action-reaction that occurs.

Walking in a circle, watch and pick up the tempo and mannerisms of the walk of each person progressively. Then, focusing on no particular person, try to establish a group tempo. Change the tempo; speed it up; slow it down; try to let it happen as a group phenomenon, rather than as the result of any one person's action.

Finally, begin with an environment of objects in space; add sound, light, people, and costumes, and stir. Let the "stew" evolve as it will.

6

Choreography

CONCEPT: Choreography is the process of selecting and forming movement into a dance, designing the action to satisfy a particular intent.

Your experiences so far in the medium of movement and the elements of time, space, and energy have been for the purposes of developing sensitivity and awareness and exploring the various materials of dance. The experiences can be viewed also as approaches to choreography. In completing the experiences and solving the movement problems so far presented, you have been going through the choreographic process in miniature. You have explored, improvised, and set movement patterns that could be repeated. What remains is to expand each of these explorations, improvisations, and patterns into dances of sufficient length and depth to satisfy you as a choreographer and others as audience.

1. Choreography involves the processes of exploration, improvisation, selection, and organization.

You are already acquainted with these processes from your previous experiences. In *exploration,* you find ways to do that which you have already decided to do. For instance, if you want to do a study of "stop and go," you might explore all the ways of stopping and going that you can think of and then select from these the ways that best suit your purpose. Again, if you want to get from a low wide position to a high narrow one in the middle of a dance, you could explore all the ways possible until you found the way that was right or most effective for your needs. Exploration goes on as a series of disconnected trials in search of material of predetermined nature.

Improvisation is a spontaneous forming, a continuous sequential growth of movement and events out of the motivating idea. It is a process of letting things happen, rather than intellectually predetermining what will occur. From the improvisation, you may sense and remember things that you will use as movement and ideas for choreography. Improvisation can give you ways of developing already chosen materials or of progressing in sequences. It can

Selection of shapes and relationships.

present you with exciting shapes, rhythms, and relationships that you will make use of or build on in choreography.

From your explorations and improvisations, you make a *selection* of material appropriate for dance. This selection can be based on intellectual reasoning, but more often it will simply come about intuitively. Reason has its place in science, but art is better served by intuition. You sense materials as important and you feel an order of movement as inevitable.

Finally, you will *organize* movement, sequences, and relationships according to what seems to be the right progression for your dance. The most careful and adequate forming of the dance will come only out of the most thorough acquaintance with the movement materials. Many times initial movements will have inherent in them the form for the whole dance. The organization of a dance can come about by an intellectual choice and ordering of parts. It can come about organically, with movement growing naturally out of previous movement in a sequential development. Or, it can come about as a combination of these two methods. You will develop form by intuition, by your sensing of the way the dance should progress. You might also develop form by chance, by selecting a possibility out of a hatful of choices.

Organization implies more than just arbitrarily stringing movements together. You will work, arrange and rearrange, improvise and explore, combine and recombine until you find a sequence that makes a kind of nonverbal sense to you. It implies that you have made the connection between movement and the meaning that this movement has for you, and the meaning is developed and extended by this particular order of movement. The movement is no longer sensed purely in its mechanics, but has meaning for you, makes you feel a certain way.

2. Choreographing is a way of getting to know yourself.

Your work as a composer of dances cannot begin too early, and should never be saved until you think that your technical development is complete. Make your mistakes early and profit from them. Each movement study you choreograph teaches you a new lesson, not only about composition, but also about the body you inhabit. Choreography is just as important for technical growth as it is for creative growth. You will demand certain skills of yourself to satisfy your choreography, and will possibly be harder on yourself than anyone else will be.

3. The reason for composing, the movement materials, and the method of working all influence the final product — the dance.

Whether you are choreographing for one dancer or for many, you will find these things to be true: first, you need a motivation for the dance. In class, this may be as simple as being told by your instructor to create a dance. This assignment may be further qualified by specific limits as to subject, length, quality, and other details. You may simply have an inner need to choreograph a dance, and be self-directed in accomplishing it. In any case, whether the motivation comes from an inside or outside source, you have an image or thought about the dance. You may be able to put your thought into words, or it may be nonverbal, coming to life only in movement. You improvise for movement materials that form it for you. Consequently, you have an idea about how that thought might manifest itself in movement. How many dancers will it need? What speed? What dynamics? What quality have you discovered or decided upon? Finally, you decide on how best to start working so that your image will take shape. The method of working strongly influences the final form of the dance, as each dance takes its own unique form.

Some dances will follow a predetermined literal course. There may be a comment that you want to make. This requires much intellectual work, thinking about the parts that are essential for a sense of the whole, about characters, sequences of events building toward resolution or climax — how you see it ending.

Other dances will begin and *grow* mostly through the interaction of intuition and movement. These are dances that are simply about movement: movement that is like "slipping off the air" as Trisha Brown said about "Glacial Decoy"; high-energy repetitive movement that is hypnotic in its effect as in Laura Dean's

"Drumming"; movement that is pedestrian, everyday stuff, or that is joyfully, intentionally dancey; or that which is capricious, whimsical, and intended to keep the audience on their toes. These dances may develop organically, rather than intellectually right out of a kinesthetic sense of events in sequence, or more formally through the use of theme and variation — something familiar but still interesting seen in a new light, or in a different direction, or on a different level.

Learning Experience

See "There Is a Time" by José Limón (on the film Language of Dance) *as an example of the rich use of theme and variation. Contrast how this looks and feels with one of Grahams' dramatic dances, "Night Journey" or "Appalachian Spring," and with one of the meditative dances of Laura Dean, "Spinning Dance" (on the* Beyond the Mainstream *tape).*

Some dances will be suitable for only one person; others will require a group to satisfy their intent, to make the strongest design statement. There are as many possible approaches and procedures with choreography as there are choreographers and dancers.

The method of working in solo choreography is determined by its motivation. You may design your dances as solos, either for yourself or for a dancer who seems to have the potential capacity to give what is needed to your dance and with whom you have good rapport. There are special things to be considered when choreographing for a solo dancer. You need to keep in mind that the single dancer must maintain consistent interest so as to hold the stage without monotony throughout the length of the dance. This means more complex movement than would be advisable in a group dance, and more careful selection of pungent moments of movement.

In working on a solo, it is very tempting for the choreographer to overuse the mirror because there are no other dancers on whom one can see the movement. This can be a dangerous procedure. Mirror-fed minds tend to deal mainly with shape, to the exclusion of other equally important elements such as motion, speed, and space. This crutchlike dependence on the mirror is the result of an attempt to get outside yourself to see what the movement looks like. Try instead to get outside yourself kinesthetically — that is, to know through muscle sensation what you look like visually.

The *free improvisation* method of composing starts from the broadest possible base and works toward the more specific. This is one way to start when you have no more concrete vision than the fact that you want to do a dance, or that you simply want to move. You begin by improvising freely, with no limitations, until some motion, shape, feeling, or other quality arrests you. That is your beginning, your seed from which the dance will grow. You continue improvising, selecting motion that seems to work and to be in harmony with the beginning seed.

When you work with a *limited problem,* already having a vision in mind, whether it be your own creation or an assigned exercise, you have a more specific basis from which to start composing. Choosing a quality of movement on which to concentrate automatically eliminates many others. Consequently, your preliminary improvisation is shortened because it is more specifically directed toward your vision. You try and discard, and finally select, movements that are true to your image, which keep the quality of your original image without reiterating it to the point of boredom. The stronger your image to begin with, the more quickly the composition will fall into place.

Be open, however, to the possibility of your vision altering before your very mind's eye. This frequently happens − an accidental occurrence may prove more interesting than the original idea. If this should happen, do not hesitate to drop the first and pursue the second. Dance compositions, like improvisations, seem to have a will of their own, and sometimes they simply will not be forced. If you let them develop naturally, you are more likely to end with a complete, organic dance.

Often something apart from the dance itself, some *outside stimulus,* will start the spark of creativity burning. Sometimes it is a particular sound or accompaniment that might lend itself well to dance. Sometimes it is a prop or a costume or an unusual physical environment. These considerations narrow the limits in which you have to work, but they also may make things more difficult for you. Because they constitute an influence that is in a way limiting to the motion, the dance will have to conform to that limitation. It can no longer go its merry way without relating to the stimulus that brought it into being in the first place.

Group choreography introduces more complexities. If your idea requires greater numbers of people to make its statement, there will be greater possibilities for building, for contrast, for harmony, for saying many things more powerfully than a single dancer can do, and perhaps even greater problems. There are at least several considerations necessary in working with a group.

The more people in your group dance, the more you need to simplify the choreography. A movement is amplified in proportion to the number of people performing it. If 20 people on a stage are all doing something different, no movement stands out, and the viewer may be hopelessly confused. A group dance needs careful pruning of extraneous movements so that the movements that are selected say very clearly what you wish them to say.

For the less experienced choreographer, it is a wise move to stay out of the group dance you are composing − or, if you must dance in it, get someone else to take your place during rehearsal so you can back off from the dance and see what is happening. In this capacity you serve as the "outside eye," and are better able to judge the workability of each phrase than you would be if you were in the midst of it. The "outside eye" is even more of a necessity in a group dance

Choreographing with group sense.

than in a solo, due to the complexity of spatial relationships and the impossibility of kinesthetically sensing anyone's movement but your own.

The motivation of the dance determines method and materials for a group choreography. In *free improvisation,* you simply turn your dancers loose with instructions to improvise on no particular subject, and wait for something to happen. When it does, seize the moment and try to have your dancers repeat it. If they can, and you like it, then you have a seed around which the rest of the dance can build. The dancers then continue to improvise with an image in mind of what they are working toward, and hopefully the dance goes on. This is probably the most haphazard way to work, and is usually most successful with experienced improvisers. It takes a while to get "tuned in" to a group; and even when things begin working, it is difficult to recall and reproduce them. It can be a very exciting way to work, however, as the resulting dance is often as much of a surprise to the choreographer as it is to anyone else.

Setting a *skeleton problem* uses improvisation, too, but this is a little more directed than free improvisation. You, as the choreographer, have an image of what you would like to see and, as well as you are able, try to communicate this image to the dancers. They then have some framework around which to begin improvising — some straw in the wind to which they can cling. As before, you then select the moments that seem to fit in with your image, ask your dancers to recall them, and gradually set them into a firm sequence. The more clearly you can describe your image, the less time will be wasted as your dancers try to discover what it is you want from them.

Still more closely directed is the *partial improvisation*, in which you give your dancers prepared sequences of movement, but also allow them sections in which to improvise. You establish the quality of the movement you would like to see, and they may improvise with it in time, space, and dynamics. In the finished dance, these sections may still be improvised to some degree, or they may jell during rehearsal so that they are nearly always performed in the same way.

The advent of the portable video camera and the videocassette recorder (VCR) makes it possible to make on-the-spot tapes of group improvisations. These in turn can be played back immediately, so dancers (and the budding choreographer) can see exactly how movement will appear in performance. Tapes can also be used to reinforce in the dancers' memories what they have performed, so the problem of forgetting what has happened in an improvisatory setting can be overcome.

In the *totally structured* way of working, you give your dancers every movement they are to do, in the sequences in which they are to be done. There is no room for improvisation; the dancers just learn what you are teaching. This, of course, necessitates a great deal of work on your part prior to rehearsals with your dancers, so that you are sure to have something to give them. You will have gone through the improvisation, exploration, and selection process yourself before confronting them. Although the forming process and order of the materials may occur when and as you see the movements being danced, it would be grossly unfair for you to ask dancers to stand around and wait while you think about the basic materials. Presenting a set structure often saves time in rehearsals, but it cannot take advantage of the spontaneous moments that often happen in improvisation.

Try many different methods of working. Although you may ultimately find one or two that are more suitable to you, you will gain from the experience of trying them all.

4. Choreographic process is individual to each choreographer and each dance.

What has been said is about all anyone can tell you about the making of dances. There is no set of rules, no progression of steps, not even an order of processes that anyone can recommend to you that will work each time. How you proceed will be a matter of your own intuition and your own sense of rightness.

You will work intuitively or intellectually, and probably some of each. You will work subjectively or objectively, sometimes being in the movement, involved only in its feel, and other times out of it, trying to see it from the point of view of the observer. You may discover that if you preplan and decide ahead of the movement what and how you are going to move, you will limit your spontaneity and the ease with which the movement flows. You may also miss the opportunity to discover something brand new that just happens to you without anticipation. You will discover at what point in the process you must look at your

Choreographer directing her work.

work objectively, to give it direction, to see what it is you have and how you can progress — to define the basis on which you will keep or throw materials away. You will find at what point you can do this without its being a detriment to the spontaneity and flow of your work, and at what point you must do this or lose the form of the dance to unrelated wanderings because you have not yet defined your direction.

Developing discrimination facilitates the process of choreography. You will grow tremendously in awareness and intuition as you see and evaluate your own and others' choreographies. The more experience you have, the more discriminating you will become.

You will have already sensed your own studies as exciting, as important to you in some way, or somehow lacking in the essential qualities. You will have seen and evaluated other studies. Hopefully, you will have sensed for yourself and discussed as a group what it is about these studies that you like, what you consider good, exciting, and stimulating, and why certain studies are dull, ordinary, and not so exciting or meaningful. Perhaps you have had insights into the "whys" of a thing being new and fresh, captivating and moving, creative and original, completely absorbing. From these insights, you should be better able to find those qualities for yourself in your own dances.

The important thing is that you work, that you choreograph, that you make dances; that you continue to evaluate your experiences, your dances, and the dances of others; and that you learn from your own reactions and those of others how you can better or more effectively fulfill your dance ideas.

Experiences in other art media will enhance your work in choreography. While you are working and learning, you may want to surround yourself with other art products and immerse yourself in other art experiences. Read what Martha Graham and Mary Wigman have to say about their choreographic experiences. Read what other artists in other areas have written about their creative processes. Picasso and Paul Klee are articulate in their descriptions. Giacometti mentions the occasional frustration and lack of surety all artists experience. Be comforted. Brewster Ghiselin's *The Creative Process* relates the experiences of artists and scientists in the act of creating. Read and reread them, for what they say may not make sense to you just now, while at another stage in your development it may be as clear to you as dawn.

Talk to other people going through the same processes and problems. Listen to what your instructor has to suggest to you. You will sort out from their insights things that contribute to your understanding. Attend concerts and plays, listen to music, read poetry, and visit museums. Experience fully, and later reflect on your reactions and try to understand them.

Learning Experiences

Begin with Martha Graham's dance film, Night Journey, *and study carefully the structure of the story of Jocasta. What function does the chorus serve? What is the effect of the seer? How are all the parts unified, not only in story line, but in movement? In costume, set, and prop? How is each part related to the others?*

Attend a concert of Alwin Nikolais, or watch one of his television films. Experience the sensory magic of motion, sound, light, and color in a theatrical whole. How is his work different from Graham's?

See, experience, and evaluate as much dance as you can and, most important, do your own choreography. Choreograph continually, a study a day if possible; it is like practicing anything in which you would like to acquire a skill. At this point, you must take full responsibility for yourself and your work, you must learn through painful trials and errors, through jubilant revelations and insights. The amount of experience you have in dance is equivalent to the amount you will grow. This is up to you.

Each of you will eventually find your own way of proceeding. You will set your own individual problems, decide on your own ideas or first movement, find your own method of approaching choreography and progressing, and define a standard of taste. Then, lo and behold, once you think you have found the way, you will discover that each dance has a mind of its own, and that you have changed a little in your ideas. This is the difficulty and frustration, the excitement and joy, of art. It is a process not yet scientifically understood or rationally explainable. It requires patience for, and tolerance of, its vagueness and obscurity. It will have its depressions and frustrations, its enlightenments and exaltations; all this you can truly anticipate. Have no illusions.

5. The dance is mounted in theatrical elements to enhance and emphasize the desired effect.

At a certain point in your development, you will be pleased enough with your choreography to consider it a worthwhile experience for an audience. You will be concerned with dance in its ultimate state — as a performing art. As an art, dance occurs in a particular environment. Environment refers to all the theatrical elements that make up the total presentation on a stage — the costumes, props, sets, lights, accompaniment, and program titles. They are those elements that heighten the experience for the viewer. They provide the magic of the stage that helps to create the illusion necessary for the art to exist as other than everyday activity. In the theatre situation, they support and intensify the dance idea.

Theatrical elements serve to enrich the experience of the viewer through an increase in sense activity. Lights will ensure the seeing of the right images, support the mood in rays and colors, help to isolate or pull together, to lift, press down, or emphasize. Sets have a significance for the dance design. They change its shape in space, supply mass, bulk, shape, and texture, intensifying or adding contrast to those already present in the movement. Props are often necessary in carrying out the full meaning of the dance. Perhaps more often they serve to extend movement lines and shapes and to emphasize qualities. When props and sets are used symbolically, they are used in the sense of drama. As such, they require additional interpretive thought on the part of the viewer. This may detract from involvement with and enjoyment of the experience of motion. Keep this in mind if you choose to use props in this way.

Costumes, while identifying period and character in drama, serve in dance more to extend the quality of a movement or accentuate parts of the body. They have the potential to create line and shape, to provide interest through their texture and color, and to support movement definitions in their line, weight, and motional qualities. They not only emphasize visual aspects, but many times provide sensations of touch through their texture and weight, thus involving a fuller sensuous response of the audience.

Music or sound accompaniment stimulates a third sense — hearing. It can intensify a mood or create an aural atmosphere in which dance can happen. It can, if the choreographer desires, even produce a sense of conflict by being opposite to the timing or quality of the dance. In giving an auditory dimension to the sensory experience of the dance, it further enriches and deepens it.

None of these elements should be added after the dance is completely formulated, however. They are conceived along with the dance, as an integral part of it. They must be organically necessary to the totality of the work. These

The magic of theatre.

elements actually affect the movement, so you must work with them in the process of learning and choreographing the dance. If this is not done, the dance may suddenly change when you add other elements. These elements should facilitate, and not oppose, the desired effect.

Sound, in particular, is influential in the effectiveness of the dance. Of all the elements, music is probably the most important in its influence on not only the dancers and audience, but also on the dance. It has the power to change the overall effect of the dance, and to irritate or to soothe the audience as it experiences the dance. In searching for dance accompaniment, then, be careful to find something suitable, something similar in mood and time to your dance. Take plenty of time to listen, and be willing to wait for that which is *most* effective. As in your choice of movement for dance, don't be too easily satisfied.

It would be nice to have music written for your choreographies, but that presents special problems of its own. Nevertheless, you may be lucky enough to find faculty or students in your music department who would welcome the chance to compose for dance. Many times, they feel it extends them in their vocabulary of sound and rhythm. You can at least talk to the music department faculty about the particular sound needs for your choreography. They can often suggest just the right composer or piece to meet your style, time, and tensional requirements. Don't hesitate to visit the college record library and record stores, and tune your radio to good music. Your familiarity with what is available will greatly facilitate the selection of accompaniment.

There may be times when it seems much easier simply to put a record on the phonograph and dance to it. This is good therapy, and you may even come up with something worthwhile by following the music's rhythms and form, or by being excited by its mood. This excitement, however, comes from an external motivation rather than from your own inner motor impulse. Here the dance accompanies the music, rather than the other way around. Some music, of course, is not too adaptable. Many pieces are so complete and powerful in themselves that a dance does little more than irritate by distracting from the music. Even professional companies have trouble performing dances to Bach masses, which are already adequate in themselves.

Do not overlook the possibilities of using nonmusical sounds such as voice, words, percussion, electronic sound, and even everyday noises for accompaniment. Their looser structure sometimes allows greater freedom in combining sound and movement.

The title of a dance in the program is very influential in affecting audience reaction. With the choreography complete, and its staging planned, what will you call your dance? This can be a problem. Your title can mislead viewers, as well as help them in understanding your dance. If there is something specific that you as a choreographer want to get across, perhaps you will insist that your audience see this in the dance. You will title it accordingly, giving people a point of view from which to see the dance. In this case, there are problems. If the title is definitive, it may lead viewers to expect certain definite thing, because of their personal associations. They may be disappointed in your interpretation, or they may be distracted from the movement by searching for the representation of the idea. They may never see the dance if they are so busy intellectually trying to figure it out in relation to its title.

This is probably why so many modern artists are content with titles like *Study in Blue* or *Number 7.* Here, observers are free to let their imaginations loose, and are not trapped into trying to find something which just isn't there. Usually, one doesn't ask of *Symphony No. 9,* "What is your meaning?" It is enough simply to enjoy the sound, harmonies, and structure.

Since most dance deals with nonliteral things and with movement ideas, choreographers often give titles of implication, of suggestion or atmosphere, as possible springboards to send the imagination of the viewer into this particular experience of movement. Perhaps it is better if a title simply identifies a dance, as a name identifies a person. What set of words can possibly contain a human personality or the motional content of a choreography?

7

Performance

CONCEPT: Performance is the final step in the choreographic process.

Once the dance is formulated and rehearsed, it will be shown, as the purpose of dance is to share it with others. Granted, there is tremendous self-satisfaction in creating choreography, but dance is by nature a performing art and fulfills its true function only when presented before people. Certainly you may dance just for your own enjoyment, but ultimately you will perform, whether it be for your own classmates, for your instructor, or for a theatre audience. To these people you have certain responsibilities, both as a dancer and as a choreographer. You are dealing with art, and this automatically means that your standards are high. They should be no different from those of the professional — to present the best work of which you are capable.

One can say that a dance is a series of transactions. The series begins with the experienced or imagined feeling of the choreographer. It is felt as a kind of restless excitement until given a plan of motion. This vision is given substance and visual existence by the dancer. It is the dance which is the link between the choreographer and the dancer, and between the dancer and the audience. And the audience, of course, is the final link in the chain.

1. The presence of an audience demands the greatest fulfillment of the performance.

The nature of the audience affects the existence of the choreography. The people in your audience arrive at your performance in various states of mind, and they see different things in that performance. They bring minds accustomed to thinking verbally, and what you are presenting to them is an essentially nonverbal art. They may also bring ideas about what they expect to see. The more firmly fixed these ideas, the greater your chance of disappointing them if you do not deliver what they expect. They bring with them their lifetime collection of associations and memories and their habit of mentally organizing and connecting new experiences and meanings with those they have had in the past. They bring with them the tendency of the educated mind to search out literal meaning in everything it sees.

It would be ideal if your audience's minds were uncluttered by old associations and by preset ideas of excellence. You would like the audience to see your work clean and pure, without past judgments clouding their vision. The experience you bring them should be like the first marks on fresh snow. Unless you dance for day-old babies, this will never be the case. The next step, then, is to provide your audience with an experience that is as crystal-clear and new as possible, and hope it will move them past their prejudices.

The choreographer has a responsibility to help the audience toward a new experience. Whether the audience be your own small group of friends or paying customers in a theatre, they have one thing in common: they expect to be stimulated in some way by what you do. Your responsibility as both a choreographer and performer is to see that they are stimulated. You may do this in a number of ways. You may arouse them emotionally, or you may provide them with a pleasant sensuous experience, give them some intellectual fodder, or even make them downright angry. The point is to give them an experience they have not had before.

The audience is responsive to the dance-theatre experience in a number of ways. Viewers are impressed visually with the shape, color, and motion that they see on the stage. They are aware of sounds, whether they be accompanying sounds or the sounds the dancers themselves make. They also vicariously live the motional experience of the dancer. They actually feel muscularly, to a slight degree, the same things the moving dancer is feeling.

These are essentially sensory responses to the dance experience. At the same time, the viewers are probably responding intellectually too, dredging up past associations and trying to apply them to the present situation. Since dance is first a sensory experience, you may as a choreographer deal with the strictly sensory aspects of your work, and leave the intellectualizing to the audience. Since each viewer will react differently anyway, by virtue of having different past memories, there is nothing that would be universally applicable.

The choreographer's responsibility, then, is to clear the channels of any extraneous associations as much as possible, so that the viewer may have a new experience. This would mean avoiding anything that has a strong symbolic tie with the past — sentimental music, hackneyed postures of emotional states, or recognized symbols like crosses, flags, and other objects, unless you are using these elements to evoke a specific response. By dealing with the abstract elements of his art, the choreographer leaves the audience free to enjoy the basic sensory experience, or to find their own meaning in it, be it abstract or literal. Abstract meaning is a perfectly valid and real outcome of dance. There are qualities of ideas and images that cannot be expressed verbally; these ideas *mean* abstractly, not literally.

The dancer has a responsibility to give the audience a full and clear experience of the dance. The audience sees what the choreographer has to say through the dancer. As the dancer, you can best serve the choreographer and the audience by becoming transparent — by letting the choreography shine through you. When your ego intrudes — when the audience is more aware of "you dancing" than it is of the motion itself, when you wear the movement like a decoration adorning your outer surface — then you clutter up the vision and the audience can no longer see the dance clearly.

The presence of the performer.

On the other hand, you have a certain responsibility to be an ingratiating performer. Part of the viewers' pleasure is in identifying kinetically with the dancer in motion, and you will make this identification hard if you present a cold and austere or in some way negative figure. There is a delicate balance between selflessness and the denial of the self.

There is a danger of clouding the choreographic issue not only with the self, but also with dramatic attitudes imposed on the choreography. If there is drama in the choreography, it will be inherent in the movement. You will not have to slap it on like a final coat of paint. When you color a movement with an emotional attitude, you immediately direct the viewers' attention down a particular avenue of thought and rob them of the opportunity to explore other avenues.

Your foremost duty, then, is to present the choreography to the audience without editorial comment. Consider yourself, instead, as the vehicle that carries the choreography to the audience. By devotion to the motion and not to what you think the motion means, you eliminate the middle man and let the audience perceive the dance directly. The concept of the dancer as interpreter of the choreography implies that the choreographer is speaking in a language audiences cannot understand without a translator, and you have often heard that something always gets lost in the translation.

Performers have maintained from time immemorial that all audiences are different and that it is necessary to play to each differently. All this is certainly true. An audience of children is different from an audience of social club members or an audience of other dancers. They will all react differently to you, and you to them. Because of the vast variations in audience composition, there is nothing that could begin to prepare you, the performer, for all the situations you may encounter. Sensing the makeup and mood of an audience is a skill that comes only after many, many performances before many types of audiences. Seize every opportunity you have to perform, even if the performing conditions sound a little dismaying. Perhaps your greatest moment of growth will come when you have to adjust to dancing on a stage the size of a bath mat, in your practice tights because your costumes got lost, to the tune of the friendly janitor's kazoo because your tape recorder broke down, for an audience of six.

Performance nerves — or in plain English, fear — is always present to some degree, and it can be either crippling or stimulating. It may so shatter you that your physical and psychical control are destroyed, or it may sharpen your energies and sensitivities so that you give the performance of your lifetime. Again, only repeated performances will teach you to deal with this problem, and no one can give you any really helpful advice on how to meet it. One can only say that the stress of performance intensifies everything. Turn your concentration to careful articulation of the motion, rather than to yourself, your nerves, and fears, and it will be motion that will be magnified for the audience — not your shaking knees.

An easiness in the face may help you to develop calmness. If you are unaccustomed to wearing a pleasant, open face when you dance then you had better practice it. Use rehearsal time for this; the night of the performance is a little late to begin. You simply have to concentrate on too many other things.

What if you make a mistake? Or even fall down? Quite honestly, the world will not come to an immediate halt. The important thing is to spare the audience the discomfort of your embarrassment. The audience is simply not interested in seeing your fears or your remorse. An attitude of confidence in performing can not only set you up in a frame of mind to help you deliver a good performance, but it can also smooth over any hitches that may occur.

The theatre situation must be clarified to provide the most magical experience for the viewer. The physical environment for dancing certainly influences the effect of the performance. In actual performance, the technical details of light and sound, hopefully, will be taken care of by at least one other person whose responsibility it is to see that all these things work properly. It is important that you, as a dancer or choreographer, find a capable, responsible, sensitive person to stage your dance, and make it perfectly plain to this person exactly what you want. To ensure the best result, know and use the proper terminologies for lights, sets, and directions on stage. Once these technical details are established and under control, you can forget about them and concentrate on what you, the dancer, can do with your performing environment.

The stage space may seem a fixed element to you, but it is really most hospitable to change. You are capable of altering the appearance of that space by the manner in which you treat it (see Chapter 4). A small stage can be made to seem infinite if you project your movement out beyond the space around you. You can do this through eye focus, through subtle extensions of motion, and

The image the audience sees.

through extension of the psyche. You can make the illusion of space that you create crash through the walls that enclose that tiny stage. Or, because of the nature of the dance, you may wish to play the movement in proportion to the actual size of the stage. This may mean treating it more intimately and inviting the audience "in" to the space, rather than projecting it out to them.

On the other hand, a large stage may be treated projectionally to take advantage of its spaciousness, or to tone it down if the space is such that it overwhelms your dance. By your focus on the motion, you may either send it out into the space or illusionally pull the boundaries of that space down to manageable size.

In any case, your audience will see what you want it to see, if you have sufficient skill. They may see a real space expand or contract. They may see a space with a density as thick as glue, or as thin as outer space. You control the space, so to a great degree, you control what the audience sees.

2. Dancers have a responsibility to each other to realize a coordinated effort and effect.

Unless you plan to dance nothing but solos all of your life, you will often find yourself a member of a group dance. In order to preserve sanity and make the experience as pleasant as possible for all concerned, you will want to be mindful of your responsibility to your fellow dancers.

The rehearsals will be the most trying times, particularly the early ones when the dance is beginning to take shape. Approach each rehearsal professionally, even though you may not be a professional yet. Come to the rehearsal sufficiently early to get your mind and body ready to work. Warm up your instrument and be ready to begin at the time set. Learn to discipline yourself to work during the time set aside for it. Wasting other people's time is inexcusable. If you have spatial problems with other dancers, or if there is a movement discrepancy, work these problems out efficiently, pleasantly, and preferably on your own, not the choreographer's, time.

Always try to rehearse "full out" — that is, just as you intend to perform, with every motion getting its full complement of energy. Not only will this build your physical stamina, but it will also heighten your own familiarity with the dynamics. You cannot "mark" through every rehearsal and expect to know how to execute the movement dynamically in performance. In addition, other dancers are taking energy cues from you, and it is impossible to achieve any kind of group rapport if there is one dead spot on the stage.

Finally, the business of group rapport is probably the most important of all, and you must work at it constantly. It is a state of awareness of the total environment and a communication that exists between the dancers, almost like a charge of electricity. You are sensitive to the motion, the timing, and the dynamics of the other dancers, and you adjust your own accordingly. If you fail to do so, you stand out as a jarring note that seems incongruous with the rest of the ensemble. When you are in this state of almost telepathic communication, you are ready for any untoward event.

3. The dancer has the responsibility to be the instrument of the choreographer.

Choreographers work in different ways, and hopefully you will have the opportunity to work with many of them. Though you are the raw material with which choreographers work, and therefore subject to their will, your duties go beyond just appearing at rehearsal to "do the steps." The extent of your contribution will vary according to the way each choreographer works. If a choreographer asks you to improvise around an idea, do so with all your creative skill. If another gives you every movement in the dance and expects to see the movements reproduced exactly, do so with accuracy. If a third choreographer asks for your suggestions, feel free to give them – constructively, of course. Ultimately, the responsibility for the success or failure of the work is on the choreographer's shoulders. Although you may disagree with a choreographer's ideas, it is not your place to correct them. You are the instrument, not the choreographer's conscience.

Try to keep your body and spirit alive and your energy up throughout the rehearsal, no matter how tired you may be. A "full out" rehearsal of a movement is doubly important to the choreographer, who cannot really see if a movement works if it is not fulfilled dynamically.

Once you have learned the movement, your work is just beginning. In the studio alone, you spend hours with yourself and with the choreography. You examine each movement to see what its character is – what quality to bring out in performance. You discover where the phrases break naturally. You find the climax of the entire piece. You practice subtleties of performance, nuances that distinguish the dancer from the hack.

You perform. You make the vision that was in the mind of the choreographer come alive. You allow the audience to see through you to the choreography, to the motion. If you can do this, then you have faithfully discharged your duty to the choreographer.

4. The dancer has the responsibility of integrity in recreating the dance.

When the final moment of truth, the performance, comes, you, the dancer, are left with two things – yourself and the choreography. Let there be no mistake as to which is the more important. A dedicated giving over of one's self to the movement is necessary to involve the audience directly in the choreography. It is only by total devotion to the motion, and to the quality therein, that a dancer can make a clear communication of the material to the audience.

5. The dancer may have the privilege of pleasing the audience.

You have come to the final link in the series of transactions. You present the dance. The audience receives it; and it goes one step further. The audience doesn't just take the experience in and keep it. There is a response, sometimes very subtle, but a response — a particular kind of energy that is produced and generated back to the dancer. It happens sometimes like refrigeration, sometimes like lukewarm water, and sometimes — if you are very lucky — like the radiance of open love and acceptance. It is for that moment that you wait.

Learning Experiences
1. *See and experience a modern dance concert, of professional level if possible, and write a critique of it, evaluating and discussing it in terms of points mentioned in this section on performance.*
2. *Choreograph and perform a dance for an audience. Evaluate the experience from your point of view and from that of the audience.*

8

Self-evaluation

CONCEPT: Self-evaluation is an integral part of the creative art process.

Concluding this brief episode of the longer journey, you might look back, reflect on the experience, and, having a sense of growth and change, wonder how to measure your accomplishments. Those directing your other dance experiences will evaluate your progress in terms of their own values and how you measure up to them, giving criticisms and suggestions worth attending to. However, the integral process of artistic evaluation is self-imposed and self-motivated: the dancer/choreographer looks at the work in terms of personal artistic tastes and performance standards. Ultimately, you are the only one who will know what goals you set for yourself and how well you achieved them.

You might have set yourself certain technical challenges: to lengthen the suspended moment of your leap, to be secure in the control of an off-center balance, to smoothly accomplish a low, slow turn on one foot. You will know you have succeeded when the motional patterns feel right to you: a turn will feel centered and complete instead of off-balance and falling apart before it's ended; a leap will feel airborne, evoking the excitement of suspension when it arrives at the magical image of flight. Meanwhile, until this happens, dance advisers can provide many helpful cues to sharpen your awareness and give greater control in these tasks.

You might also have set yourself some very objective tasks: to extend your leg three inches higher, to hold it in extension five seconds longer, to widen your sitting position three floor boards, to put the palms of both hands flat on the floor in a standing position with straight knees. There might be satisfaction in accomplishing these things, and it would be expected that these accomplishments might give greater facility and movement potential to you as a performer. In dance activity, however, the "how high, how far, how fast, how many times" is always less important and less interesting than the mere determination of "how." If the high leg extension occurs at the expense of the alignment of the rest of the body (lifting also in that hip, buckling in the supporting leg), if it is accomplished with visible effort, if it is done just to show how high you can extend it, it is meaningless and lacking in any real dance quality.

Similarly, the fact of a wide and deep second position stretch is simply a fact, unless the "hows" are attended to: legs extended, and rotated out, the torso pulling up and out rather than collapsing in and down, freedom from distorting tension in the shoulders and neck. Check yourself on the "how" of your technical accomplishments, getting help from experts until you develop your own awareness sufficiently.

You might also challenge your understanding of basic concepts of dance by moving given patterns of:

1. Locomotion. Example: run, run, hop, run, run, leap, run, hop, run, leap, run, jump in 6/8 time.
2. Rhythm. Example: 4/4.

3. Energy. Example: sustained (5 counts), swinging (3), percussive (2), sustained (2).
4. Space. Example: medium horizontal (3 counts), low rolling (4), high vertical (1).

Your dance adviser will check your performances for accuracy: are you differentiating hops from leaps from jumps? Have you accented time so that the rhythmic pattern has sharpness and clarity? Is your energy changing intensity with quality and speed? There are objective and subjective aspects of these solutions: not only that they are solved correctly, but also *how* they are solved, designed, and performed is important. Is the full body involved in, accompanying, the locomotor pattern? Is the space design interesting, pleasing, effective? How is the energy pattern performed — under control, in balance, with correctly executed plié?

Outside of examples like these, there is little else that can be submitted to objective evaluation in dance. It is always the combination of objective and subjective aspects, a clean, clear technique along with the feeling and projective qualities of the performer, that make the difference. Technique without quality can be mechanically correct but seems barely alive, as you will begin to feel. A teacher knowledgeable in the development of motor skill can give you sound criticism and advice in the area of dance technique — the only aspect of dance in which there are actual rights and wrongs, in which the body must proceed according to certain unvarying physical laws. In the long run, technique is evaluated in terms of how well it serves the choreography, not how well it displays your accomplishment of good technique.

It is the choreography that is most difficult to criticize and evaluate. There are no objective measures of its worth, no absolute rules and recipes to follow for guaranteed results. Listen to your adviser who can describe the traditional compositional values such as unity, variety, contrast, and balance, and the more contemporary aesthetic that ascribes to other values. Most important, see as much dance as possible, begin to take note of what things you like and value, what is effective and excites you, analyzing why it does and how the choreographer achieved it. It is a matter of developing your own aesthetic judgment and taste and then applying it to your own work. Evaluation of your own work makes it necessary to see it. This necessity provides one of the greatest problems for dancer/choreographers.

Difficulties arise for any artist in arriving at a point of objectivity, getting far enough away from the work to view objectively its strengths and flaws. Sculptors and graphic artists have the advantage of actual physical distance. They step back from, walk around, look down at or up into their work. Choreographers who dance their own dances are the dance, inseparable from it. It is difficult to remove themselves from the dance. Trying to catch a glimpse of the fleeting images in the mirror only causes distortion in head positions and timing, a destructive splitting of attention, and a habit of inappropriate and irrelevant focus.

Working your dance on someone else's body may give adequate visual perspective but may not be precisely what you want: the dance changes slightly in concept and feeling with each new movement personality that performs it. It will solve things nicely if you have designed your dance for the other person from the beginning, but if it is meant to be something for your own performance, then the problem continues.

A lot will depend on your kinesthetic feedback: Does the movement feel as you want it to feel? But even our own kinesthetic sense plays tricks on us. A habitual error in alignment feels perfectly natural instead of being perceived as a distortion: continually high, tense shoulders feel right but visually conflict with lifting the chest and lengthening the neck; a well-trained ankle extends automatically even when you intend to flex it. How will you check on the things that feel one way but are actually another, the discrepancies between felt and visual cues?

Most helpful perhaps is the modern miracle of videotape and instant playback. Even as a two-dimensional medium, it records dance and performance for your analysis and contemplation. Now you will identify your own technical errors and weaknesses, catch your unconscious habits and clichés of style. The tape will record your involvement (or lack of it) in improvisation, your sensitivity to and connection with other dancers and the motion occurring around you. If used from the beginning of your work in dance, sequential recordings will help you keep track of your progress in these areas, help you identify things you need to work on and want to improve.

Videotape is an invaluable aid in the choreographic process. It commits to memory those "just right" moments of improvisation that might otherwise be lost. It confirms that this "just right" moment not only feels right but looks that way, too.

As the choreography progresses, a tape reveals stronger and weaker sections, gives insight about sequences and transitions, and clarifies problems and their solutions in space design and time structure. It allows you to check and recheck selections and arrangements of material in working for the most effective form. You will actually see vagueness, inconsistency, and confusion in the choreography, and later will confirm the clarity and definition resulting from your reworking these problem areas. As the work is completed, the tape gives you a chance to sit back and perceive your work from the audience viewpoint, then to clarify and reshape it for their fullest apprehension of it. Tape will also reveal the inadequate techniques of performance that steal from the potential strength of the choreography and will let you know when these deficiencies are taken care of.

In choreographing, you will constantly evaluate the material and the form in relation to the dance idea — you'll ask yourself, "Is there a better way?" In performance, you will constantly evaluate the technique relative to the full rendering of the choreography — "Is there yet more in the choreography to be projected?" Others can give their criticisms, evaluations, and suggestions that you will accept as they seem appropriate and valid, but the final evaluation can only be yours. Ask specific questions of yourself and others about your work, and use responses of good/bad, right/wrong as cues giving direction toward improving aspects and parts, not as final judgments.

While moving your dance or viewing it on video, you might ask yourself these questions: "Am I fully realizing the movement potential of each gesture and phrase of the choreography or am I merely 'moving through' the sequences?"; "Where and why have I lost contact with the movement, lost the inner motivation for doing it fully?"; "Has it lost importance in this piece?"; "Should I keep it and perfect it, or throw it out?"; "Why do I continue to forget this part?"; "Is it unnecessary or is it out of order occurring at this time?"

"What am I actually doing in the performance of this dance that I don't know I'm doing?"; "Where are the holes in my kinesthetic awareness?"; "What personal idiosyncrasies and movement habits sneak into all my choreographies whether they're appropriate or not, intended or not?"

"Outside of all these details which have a way of calling attention to themselves, what about the whole thing?"; "Would it be interesting enough, even if I weren't dancing it, to keep me watching it closely throughout?"; "Where does it drop in interest?"; " Why?"; "Does it go for too long?"; "Is it too repetitive?"; "Should it develop more fully here, arrive at a climax sooner, or have a greater contrast somewhere else?"; "Does the end serve to intensify what's gone on before, or is it anticlimactic?"; "Does it peter out or pack a wallop?"; "Why?"; "How do I want it to end?"

How do you know these answers for sure? How will you evaluate? You proceed subjectively, on the basis of feeling. How does it feel in each part, in going from part to part, how does it feel overall? Ultimately, it is only your feeling in relation to what you see that can give you the answer to the question: "Did I do what I intended to do? Am I content that I did it in the most satisfying and effective way?"

There are other personal questions you might want to ask yourself: "Did I give as much time to this as I might have?"; "Did I go as far as I might have in the time allowed?"; "Did I find anything new instead of relying on my old clichés?"; "Did I extend and develop new movement ideas or just flash through them briefly and drop them again?"; "Did I search and find something meaningful enough that I could really get into and stay with completely or did I just dabble from the outside?"; "Did I risk anything — mostly finding out about myself?"; "Did I risk my own answer or give that known to please another?"; "Did I commit myself to this creative experience, the process of becoming?"; "Did I take the initiative and charge ahead, or just wait until I was told what to do and how to proceed, making changes in my own ideas as I heard the criticism of others?"; "Have I developed any sense of self-discipline, self-direction, self-evaluation?"; "Have I learned to stand on my own two feet — to trust my own two feet?"

There is no one who knows these answers better than you do. Did you accomplish what you set out to as a person? Did you move toward the realization of your own potential? Did you extend the range of your possibilities? Evaluation in your own terms is an integral part of the process of creative art, not unlike the process of creative living.

9

The Dance Experience and Growth

CONCEPT: The dance experience is synonymous with growth.

The end of this course may mark the end of your personal contact with dance or the beginning of a rewarding pursuit of dance, either as participant or spectator. Whether you continue to dance is not the main point. The point is that you are not the same person you were at the beginning of this course.

You cannot be the same because you have had new experiences — experiences in moving, in seeing, in creating. You have felt the stretch of a muscle, the torsion of a twist, the sensation of weight, and the fatigue of a muscle used to its capacity. You know how it feels to be upside down, to run and stop, and to be dizzy from turning.

You turned to your creative resources and found them capable of originality. You dug inside yourself and found ideas, gave those ideas physical form, and showed those forms to someone else.

You have had new experiences in seeing, because new knowledge changes the way you see. You have learned to see spatially — in line, shape, and mass. You have learned to see time — its duration and its speed. You have turned your eyes to those abstract qualities that make up motion, which make up your world. You have seen other people, other dancers, and other dances. You have seen yourself from the inside out and the outside in.

In short, you know yourself and your world a little better, and you know what it is to dance.

10

Other Sources of Information

CONCEPT: When growth overcomes inertia, it sets up a momentum difficult to stop.

Here are some suggestions for your further enrichment:

Periodicals

Contact Quarterly (quarterly) Contact Collaborations Inc., Box 603, Northampton, MA 01061.

Dance Magazine (monthly) 33 W. 60th St., New York, NY 10036.

Dance Research Journal (biannual) CORD, Dance Dept. 684 D, NYU, 35 W. 4th St., New York, NY 10003.

Readings in Dance

Banes, Sally. *Terpsichore in Sneakers: Post Modern Dance.* 2d ed. Middletown, CT: Wesleyan University Press, 1988.

Blom, Lynne and L. Tarin Chaplin. *The Intimate Act of Choreography.* Pittsburgh, PA: University of Pittsburgh Press, 1982.

_____. *The Moment of Movement.* Pittsburgh, PA: University of Pittsburgh Press, 1989.

Brown, Jean Morrison, ed. *The Vision of Modern Dance.* Princeton, NJ: Princeton Book Co., Publ., 1979.

Cohen, Selma Jeanne, ed. *The Modern Dance: Seven Statements of Belief.* Middletown, CT: Wesleyan University Press, 1966.

_____. *Dance as a Theatre Art: Source Readings in Dance History from 1581 to the Present.* NY: Dodd, Mead, 1974.

Cunningham, Merce. *Changes: Notes on Choreography*. West Glover, NY: Something Else Press, 1969.

Ellfeldt, Lois. *A Primer for Choreographers*. Palo Alto, CA: Mayfield Publ. Co., 1971.

_____. *Dance: Magic to Art*. Palo Alto, CA: Mayfield Publ. Co., 1975.

Fitt, Sally. *Dance Kinesiology*. NY: Schirmer Books, 1988.

Foster, Susan Leigh. *Reading Dancing: Bodies and Subjects in Contemporary American Dance*. Berkeley, CA: The University of California Press, 1986.

Ghiselin, Brewster, ed. *The Creative Process, A Symposium*. Berkeley, CA: The University of California Press, 1952.

Hawkins, Alma. *Creating Through Dance*. Revised ed. Princeton, NJ: Dance Horizons/Princeton Book Co., Publ., 1988.

Hays, Joan. *Modern Dance: A Biomedical Approach to Teaching*. St. Louis, MO: C.V. Mosby, 1981.

H'Doubler, Margaret. *Dance: A Creative Art Experience*. Madison, WI: University of Wisconsin Press, 1957.

Horst, Louis. *Pre-Classic Dance Forms*. Princeton, NJ: Dance Horizons/Princeton Book Co., Publ., 1987.

Horst, Louis, and Carroll Russell. *Modern Dance Forms*. Princeton, NJ: Dance Horizons/Princeton Book Co., Publ., 1987.

Humphrey, Doris. *The Art of Making Dances*. NY: Grove Press, 1962.

Jowitt, Deborah. *Time and the Dancing Image*. NY: William Morrow & Co., 1988.

Kraus, Richard and Sara Chapman. *History of the Dance in Art and Education*. 2d ed. Englewood Cliffs, NJ: Prentice-Hall, 1969.

Kreemer, Connie. *Further Steps: Fifteen Choreographers on Modern Dance*. NY: Harper and Row, Publ., 1987.

Livett, Anne. *Contemporary Dance*. NY: Abbeville Press, 1978.

Lloyd, Margaret. *The Borzoi Book of Modern Dance*. Princeton, NJ: Dance Horizons/Princeton Book Co., Publ., 1987.

Mazo, Joseph H. *Prime Movers: The Makers of Modern Dance in America*. Princeton, NJ: Dance Horizons/Princeton Book Co., Publ., 1984.

McDonagh, Don. *The Rise and Fall and Rise of Modern Dance*. NY: Outerbridge & Dientsfrey, 1970.

_____. *The Complete Guide to Modern Dance*. Garden City, NY: Doubleday & Company, 1976.

Martin, John. *Book of the Dance*. NY: Tudor Publishing Co., 1963.

_____. *The Modern Dance.* Princeton, NJ: Dance Horizons/Princeton Book Co., Publ., 1965.

Morgenroth, Joyce. *Dance Improvisation.* Pittsburgh, PA: University of Pittsburgh Press, 1987.

Nagrin, Daniel. *How to Dance Forever: Surviving Against the Odds.* NY: William Morrow & Co., 1988.

Schlaich, Joan and Betty Dupont, eds. *Dance: The Art of Production.* 2d ed. Princeton, NJ: Dance Horizons/Princeton Book Co., Publ., 1988.

Sherbon, Elizabeth. *On the Count of One: A Guide to Movement and Progression in Dance.* Palo Alto, CA: National Press, 1968.

Sorell, Walter. *The Dance Through the Ages.* NY: Grossett & Dunlap, 1967.

_____. *Dance in Its Time.* Garden City, NY: Doubleday and Company, 1981.

Turner, Margery. *New Dance: Approaches to Nonliteral Choreography.* Pittsburgh, PA: University of Pittsburgh Press, 1971.

Wigman, Mary. *The Language of Dance.* Middletown, CT: Wesleyan University Press, 1966.

Videotapes

Ailey Dances

Baryshnikov by Tharp

The Catherine Wheel (Twyla Tharp)

Hanya: Portrait of a Pioneer (Hanya Holm)

Martha Graham: Three Contemporary Dances

All available for sale from Princeton Book Co., Publ., P.O. Box 57, Pennington, NJ 08534

Walk-Around Time (Merce Cunningham) Cunningham Dance Foundation, 463 West Street, New York, NY 10014 (sale or rental)

Beyond the Mainstream: Post Modern Dance Films, Inc., 733 Green Bay Road, Wilmette, IL 60091 (sale or rental)

Films

Four Pioneers. Films, Inc. (rental)

Invention in Dance. Audio Visual Center, Indiana University, Bloomington, IN 47401 (sale or rental)

Language of Dance. Indiana University (sale or rental)

Night Journey Phoenix Films, 470 Park Ave. South, New York, NY 10016 (sale); c/o Audio-Visual Services, Kent State University, Kent, OH 44242 (rental)

Index